Eva

Congregational

# Evangelical

## and

# Congregational

**Quinta Press**

Weston Rhyn

on behalf of

**The Evangelical Fellowship of
Congregational Churches,**

Beverley

2003

**Quinta Press**

Meadow View, Weston Rhyn, Oswestry, Shropshire,
England, SY10 7RN

Visit our web-site: http://www.quintapress.com

First published 1981
Revised edition 2003
Reprinted 2004, 2008

Set in Adobe Garamond 10 on 12pt

ISBN 1  897856 19 9
ISBN–13 978 1897856 19 2

**The Evangelical Fellowship of
Congregational Churches**

PO Box 34, Beverley, East Yorkshire, England, HU17 0YY
EFCC web-site: www.efcc.org.uk

Typeset by Quinta Press and printed by Chris Fowler International

# EVANGELICAL AND CONGREGATIONAL

## 'The Principles of the Congregational Independents'

prepared by the committee of

## AN EVANGELICAL FELLOWSHIP OF CONGREGATIONAL CHURCHES

from a draft written by
Rev. Gordon T Booth, MM, BD

# CONTENTS

# FOREWORD

It is a privilege to be asked to write a foreword to this publication by the committee of An Evangelical Fellowship of Congregational Churches.

The Ecumenical Movement has not only confronted evangelical ministers and people with the need to determine afresh what the Gospel is but also what the Church is. To attempt to do the first while refusing to do the second is tantamount to maintaining that there is no necessary connection between the Gospel and the Church, and that one's evangelicalism can be justly restricted to the Gospel and not allowed to bring its effects to bear on the nature of the Church and its life.

Congregational Independency in its origin and early years would not tolerate any hiatus between the Gospel and the Church. John Owen wrote a treatise on 'The True Nature of a Gospel Church'. This book seeks to make the same link and it argues for the Biblical nature of its distinctive ecclesiology in an earnest but responsible manner. Intensity of feeling is revealed but no intolerance of spirit. This book should be read by all who are concerned that our churches today should be to the glory of God.

HYWEL R. JONES

Wrexham 1980

# SOME RELEVANT DATES

1658: THE SAVOY DECLARATION OF FAITH AND ORDER: Messengers from 120 churches met at the Savoy in London and agreed a statement of Scriptural doctrines and church order.

1662: ACT OF UNIFORMITY: After the restoration of the monarchy, Parliament passed an Act requiring all ministers to conform to the Prayer Book and the whole system of the Church of England. Some 2,000 would not do so and were turned out of their livings.

1833: DECLARATION OF FAITH, CHURCH ORDER, AND DISCIPLINE agreed at the Annual Assembly of the newly-formed Congregational Union of England and Wales.

1884: MANUAL OF CONGREGATIONAL PRINCIPLES published. Written by Dr R.W. Dale, a book frequently quoted herein and to which we are much indebted.

1967: AN EVANGELICAL FELLOWSHIP OF CONGREGATIONAL CHURCHES (EFCC) was formed.

1972: UNITED REFORMED CHURCH: About four-fifths of the Congregational Churches in England and Wales surrendered their Independency and joined with the Presbyterian Church of England to form the United Reformed Church.

*Chapter* 1

# WHO ARE THE
# CONGREGATIONALISTS?

A hundred years ago there were over 4,000 Congregational Churches in England and Wales. Now there are not many more than 500. And even those that remain may be described on the notice-board outside their buildings in various ways:— Independent Chapel, Free Church, Mission, Evangelical Congregational Church and so on.

And not all who worship in these buildings are ready to admit that they are Congregationalists. Even a Church Secretary has been heard to remark: 'Of course, I am not a Congregationalist'. Yet he would be a member of a church outside whose building the notice-board read 'Congregational Church'.

How has this sad and confused situation arisen? So far as the names are concerned, this is largely due to the long and varied history of churches of the Congregational denomination. All Congregational Churches are 'Independent'—this was the name more commonly used in earlier years: the terms 'chapel' or 'meeting house' were used to indicate that 'church' meant people rather than a building. All Congregational Churches are 'Free Churches', in the sense of not being under the authority of the State. All the old Congregational Churches were 'evangelical', in their submission to the authority of Scripture, in their dependence on the grace of God, and in their determination to 'hold forth the word of life' to a perishing world.

But what of their sad decline and of the reluctance even of officers to acknowledge their Congregationalism? To this we shall return later. First, we consider the ways in which the Church of Christ orders itself, and make a brief review of the Congregational story.

## The Ordering of the Church

All Christians must acknowledge that the Lord Jesus Christ is Head of the Church but, historically, there have been three kinds of church order, or ways in which the Church expresses that Headship and manages its affairs. These can be described as Episcopal, Presbyterian, and Independent.

The episcopal system of church government recognises a bishop who can be said to rule as a 'monarch' within the denomination. The Anglican, Roman Catholic, and Greek Orthodox Churches are examples of this. In the presbyterian system, the denomination is governed by 'presbyters' or appointed leaders meeting in a 'synod' or 'conference' drawn from many congregations. With certain modifications, the Church of Scotland, the Elim Church, the United Reformed Church, and the Methodist Church are examples of this. In Independency, it is held that each local church has 'congregated' under the Headship of Christ alone and is, therefore, independent of all or any external human control, whether this be of the State or of any other church (or group of churches or church representatives).

The Assemblies of God, the Baptist Churches, the Churches of the Fellowship of Independent Evangelical Churches, are examples of this system of church order. Congregational Churches are independent.

# Early Heroes

Congregationalists are the descendants of the first Free Church martyrs in England. In the early days of the Reformation, the 'official' Church (and therefore the State) frowned upon any dissent from its authority. But there were those who longed for far deeper reforms than the 'established' church would permit. Henry Barrowe, John Greenwood, and John Penry, all graduates of Cambridge, would not be silenced and were placed in the Fleet Prison, in the City of London. (The Congregational Memorial Hall was erected on the site. The building now erected on the site is Caroone House, which no longer has any connection with Congregationalism). From thence they were taken to be hanged at Tyburn in April and May, 1593. Their story and that of the many other separatists of Elizabeth's reign reminds us forcibly of the churches in lands where the is no religious freedom today. They were pioneers of gospel witness from the dock, openly confessing their faith in the full knowledge that it meant imprisonment and suffering. Indeed, Dr Peel, the Congregational historian, suggested that four hundred years ago, 'the largest Congregational churches were those which met in London prisons'.

The Independents were the acknowledged founders of the United States. The Visitors' Book in the parish church of the little village of Scrooby in Nottinghamshire is filled with the names of American visitors to the home of William Brewster, leader of the Pilgrim Fathers. Oliver Cromwell was an Independent and the army which rid the England of his day from the curse of arbitrary despotism was very largely an army of Independents. His government, in days of extraordinary success and influence, was a pioneer and model of toleration and administrative efficiency. Judged as one of the finest generals in the history of war, yet his supreme concerns were the worship and service of God and the spreading of the Gospel. His Congregationalist contemporary, John Owen, Vice-chancellor of the University of Oxford, ranks as one of the greatest theologians England has produced.

With the death of Cromwell and the restoration of the monarchy, there came in 1662 the Act of Uniformity compelling all ministers in the Church of England to assent to the 39 Articles of Religion and conform to the Prayer Book services. Nearly 2,000 ministers refused and were ejected from their livings. Many were Presbyterian but others became ministers to the number of Congregational Churches whose formal beginning dates from that time.

In the development of worship, it was the Congregationalist Isaac Watts, who established modern hymnology. Many consider him a finer writer of hymns than even Charles Wesley, whose prolific and poetic output makes him Watts' only possible competitor. Watts delivered the congregation from the exclusive use of the psalter, sung all too often in the forced rhymes and rhythms of the metrical psalms. Philip Doddridge, Watts' younger contemporary, was preacher, pastor, educationalist, theologian and himself a hymn-writer. High academic standards owe much to the dissenting academies at a time when the ancient universities, closed to the Non-conformist, were often hardly worthy of the name of educational establishments. In this sphere the contribution of Doddridge at his Northampton Academy was outstanding.

Later, when God blessed with revival in the Evangelical Awakening in the days of Whitefield and the Wesleys, in the main, after initial hesitation, the Independents were ready to receive and reap a blessing.

The closing decade of the eighteenth century opened the era of modern missionary enterprise. The Congregationalists of the London Missionary Society, founded only three years after the Baptist Society of Carey, provided an astonishing array of pioneers. They included Van-der-Kemp among the Kaffirs, Robert Moffat to Bechuanaland, his famous son-in-law David Livingstone to central Africa, Robert Morrison and Griffith John to China, and John Williams to the South Seas. These were worthy successors of the Congregational missionary pioneer, John Eliot of Nazeing, who joined the Pilgrim Fathers in America in 1631. He has been called the 'Father of Modern Missions' and was the first to translate the Scriptures into a heathen tongue for the purpose of missionary work.

At home the nineteenth century was the period of the exploding population that accompanied the Industrial Revolution. Moved by a passion for souls the Congregationalists of those days produced evangelists and preachers determined to search out 'every creature' and bring them the Gospel. This earnest zeal resulted in the planting of very many churches in the expanding cities and industrial towns and in the least significant villages of the countryside. They were home mission pioneers to countless places.

This concern to spread the news of salvation brought the county unions and associations into being. The Independents, who had always recognised their family identity, could not in isolation achieve their aims. Without compromising their local independency they co-operated to act effectively in a mission to 'darkest Britain'.

Even in the twentieth century Congregationalists can claim in Lionel Fletcher one of the greatest evangelists this country has ever known. Although he itinerated widely his supreme gift was in pastoral evangelism. The churches in which he ministered became the largest Congregational Churches—in Australia, his native land; in New Zealand; and, most outstandingly, in Britain. His robust soul-winning proclamation filled the three thousand seats of Wood Street Congregational Church, Cardiff, and services often began half-an-hour early when every seat was taken. His books *Mighty Moments* and *After Conversion—What?* deserve to be reprinted for the edification of the present generation.

These, then, are the Congregationalists. They are Christians who believe that each church is 'independent' of external control. They disallow the authority of the State to dictate how they should worship or serve God. They do not acknowledge the right of any other church (or group of churches or church representatives) to intervene in their affairs. They are 'congregational' because every believing and covenanted member of the local church has a part in the government of his own church. They differ from Baptists because they baptise infants as well as believers. Their essential witness is to the direct Lordship of Jesus Christ in the life of each local congregation.

Any modern Congregational church-member who denies he is a Congregationalist (though by definition and practice he is one!) may well have a misconception of the meaning of the word 'Congregational'. Or he may be unaware of the glorious heritage which is his. Or, as likely as for any other reason, he may have been ashamed of what the term 'Congregational' had come to convey to the evangelical Christian. To so many, the term denoted a denomination that had denied the truth of the Bible and lost the cutting edge of the Gospel.

## Spiritual Decline

None of the major denominations passed unscathed through the theological tribulation that spread from Germany in the middle of the nineteenth century. In due course it engulfed virtually the whole Christian world. Known variously as 'modernism' or 'liberalism', the 'social gospel' was one of its facets. Gradually the colleges of the Anglicans, Baptists, Congregationalists, Methodists and Presbyterians succumbed. The ministerial products of these colleges used the pulpit to introduce the 'new theology' to the pew. In truth it was no more than a fresh manifestation of the age-old devil of humanism and unbelief. The Baptist Charles Haddon Spurgeon's great and fruitful ministry was almost certainly shortened by the strain of the warfare in those days of the 'Downgrade Controversy'. At least his own Pastors' College preserved for many years an evangelical influence among the Baptists, particularly of the South-east. The Anglicans, too, never completely lost evangelical centres for the training of their ministers.

There was nothing new in all this. The heyday of 17th century Puritanism gave way to a period of spiritual decline. At that time the theological apostasy was known as 'Deism'. Virtually the whole of the great Presbyterian denomination and the General Baptists turned Unitarian. ('English' Presbyterians of the 19th/20th centuries were the product of invaders' from north of the Border!) But, for the most part, at that earlier period of declension, the old Independents stood firm. When the foundations were shaken around them they held fast to the rock of Holy Scripture. Some argue that even when the preacher strayed, the congregation sang the great gospel truths in Watts' hymns and remained true to the 'old paths'.

Certainly many a modern Congregationalist is saddened by the way in which his more immediate predecessors drifted with the tide, but he has no more cause for shame than his contemporaries of other denominations. There *were* churches and ministers whose testimony was unsullied by compromise. Voices *were* raised in protest at the Christ-denying utterances of the theological trend-setters. If the latest Congregational hymn book was adopted they ignored the vapid rhymings introduced into it and sang Watts and Wesley and Newton and Cowper. But they became voices crying in the wilderness. They were dismissed as theological illiterates or publicly derided in the assemblies of their denomination.

It is not easy to swim against the tide. Such men may not have walked the corridors of the increasing power of the denominational headquarters or ascended the leading pulpits of a Congregationalism which, at an earlier date, would have rejoiced in their witness. But their successors can be thankful for their fidelity. They can work to make 'Congregational' or 'Independent' an honourable term once more. Less now than for many years do we have to bear the reproach of an apostate Congregationalism. We can and should rejoice and give thanks for a distinguished lineage.

*Chapter 2*

# THE BIBLICAL NATURE OF CONGREGATIONAL CHURCHES

To the Bible-believing Christian, the Scriptures of the Old and New Testaments are the supreme authority for faith and practice. If our reason for being Congregationalists is no more than the accident of upbringing or of location and not of Scriptural conviction, we are making a mockery of our claim to a Bible-based faith. Our contention is that Independency is the system of church order and government that fully accords with the example and teaching of the New Testament. There are certain aspects of Episcopalianism which accord with Biblical churchmanship. These are found in Congregationalism. Presbyterianism has a number of features which accord with the New Testament. These, too, are found in Congregationalism. But the most essential aspects of Congregational practice are lacking in Episcopal and Presbyterian churches. To that extent, though such bodies may be Gospel-preaching and Bible-believing, we hold that they fall short of the full-orbed and divinely-ordained plan for the Church of the Lord Jesus Christ.

Dr RW Dale, in his *Manual of Congregational Principles,* provides a logical and Biblical framework for the proposition that only a Congregational Church meets the demands of the New Testament for a true church. He begins with the exposition of two fundamental principles which we expect our readers to accept without discussion.

1  *It is the will of Christ that all those who believe in him should be organised into churches.*

2  *In every Christian church the will of Christ is the supreme authority.*

It is when we reach the third principle that a great divide appears between Congregationalists and many Episcopalians and Presbyterians.

3  *It is the will of Christ that all the members of a Christian church should be believers.*

Way back in the sixteenth century, Robert Browne, the pioneer of post-Reformation Congregationalism, declared that a church must consist of 'people' and must be 'pure'. This was revolutionary thinking. To Rome the church was an institution, churches were buildings. To Browne the church comprised believers, however few. He saw that not all those who had been sprinkled in infancy by a priest, but those and those alone who had a true Scriptural faith in Christ comprised his body, his Church. Only the regenerate could be members of his Church.

It must be 'pure', without that mingling of the unsaved, which every parochial system infers.

The Reformers saw a clear distinction between the Visible and the Invisible Church. The Visible Church was the work of man—man baptised, man confirmed, man put on a church roll. Many have based their hope of salvation upon these alone. The

Invisible Church is the work of the Holy Spirit. God has called and moved and saved and he alone knows his true Church.

Dale expounds the words of Matthew 18:15–20 to insist that only Christians should be members of the Church. His argument can be summarised:

a   *The Church is constituted where there are even so few as two or three gathered together in the name of Jesus.*

b   *The function of discipline within the community of faith must be committed exclusively to those who are believers.*

c   *The power of binding and loosing implies that the members of the society are loyal to Christ.*

d   *The privilege of his presence is assured to those who are his by faith.*

As we look at the Church as it grew we see that it was as men and women became believers in Christ. When the letters were written to the New Testament churches we find them addressed to 'saints', which argues that they should live holy lives because of their faith in Christ. Paul's frequent note of thanksgiving stems from his confidence that his readers are rejoicing in the blessing of redemption through Jesus Christ.

The only plea that can be used against the Congregational insistence that all members must be believers is that it is difficult to distinguish wheat from tares. Once the great Roman Empire became at least nominally Christian it was felt that the conflict between Christianity and paganism was over and it was thought impossible to limit membership to the believer. When society is established upon Christian principles it is easy for people to count themselves Christian because of their habits of thought and worship and their moral code. Such people are not so readily discerned as lacking the essential touch of the Holy Spirit's regenerative work. However, because a task becomes difficult it is not to be shirked or regarded as impossible. The alternative is a so-called Christian church on its way back to paganism (a tendency often visible in Roman Catholicism), or on its way to obscurity as a moral or social improvement society (as so much of modern Protestantism). Some in the church of the 4th century accepted the theory that the Christian character of a degenerate Christian society might be preserved by restricting authority within it to a spiritual elite, a priesthood. But within a generation the priestly caste could be drawn from the ranks of the unregenerate and the last state would be worse than the first. Authority could now be absolute in the hands of those who professed Christianity but were in fact unbelievers.

Dale's fourth principle takes us to the very heart of the Congregational understanding of the nature of the Church.

4   *By the will of Christ all the members of a Christian church are directly responsible to him for maintaining his authority in the church.*

We may note here that the term 'Independent' may be used of a church that lacks essential characteristics of Congregationalism. It may be a church that is free of external control but yet surrenders rule and authority entirely to its officers. There are independent mission halls and assemblies that have none of the ministerial offices of the New Testament but are run by committees or even by individuals. This was not the way of the historic 'Independents'. They were Congregationalists, even though they often used the alternative title of Independent.

Two Biblical examples should be sufficient to demonstrate the authority of the whole congregation. First, in the election of an apostle to take the place of Judas the whole church shared (Acts 1:15ff). Secondly, when the administration of charitable funds required special officers for the work it was, again, the whole church who elected the 'seven'(Acts 6:2ff).

Similarly the authority to exercise church discipline is, by Matthew 18:15–20, vested finally in the whole church. When the Corinthians needed to discipline a member guilty of gross immorality, Paul urged, not the officers alone, but the whole church to excommunicate him. The church acted to punish the offender (1 Corinthians 5:2–8). Later Paul urges them to restore the penitent to fellowship. His appeal is again directed to the whole church (2 Corinthians 2:5–11).

The authority and influence of the apostles was undoubtedly great. The responsibilities of elders and deacons were obviously real and important. But it is evident in reading the New Testament that the whole congregation was thoroughly involved in ordering all the life of the church.

5   *By the will of Christ every society of Christians organised for Christian worship, instruction and fellowship is a Christian church, and is independent of external control.*

The Congregationalism of the New Testament churches assures their Independency. To exercise authority as a believing congregation it must necessarily be free of external control. Without Independency, Congregationalism is impossible.

The vital passage of Matthew 18 assures us that authority lies with the church even though it number but two or three. Its authority derives from the presence of Christ. To believers his authority is absolute. Their profession of faith declares their intention to seek to know his will and then to do it. However they may seek that knowledge, once it is known the decision is made. Their sources of information may be external to their company and they may hear wise counsel from others but, in the end, through the Scriptures and by the Spirit, he reveals his will and purpose to *them,* his people in that place. They are able to hear and to heed his voice. Since he and he alone is their Lord no external authority is required nor should be admitted.

This is precisely what we observe in the New Testament Members of the church at Jerusalem founded the church at Antioch. When the Holy Spirit selected Paul and Barnabas for the task of initiating the world-wide mission of the church there was no reference made to Jerusalem or to the apostles. The independent action of the church at Antioch was directed by God himself as they sought their Lord with prayer and fasting. Again the church at Corinth, though divided and morally in error, was called upon to obey Christ its Lord in disciplining its offending brother. The Lord used Paul the apostle to awaken the Corinthians to their responsibility to Christ but the apostle did not subvert the authority Christ had entrusted to the church. He did not assume the role the Lord had reserved for himself.

Another point must be stressed. The word 'church' is used in the New Testament either of a simple, local assembly or of the whole community of believers everywhere. Paul refers to the churches of Macedonia, the churches of Galatia, the churches throughout Syria and Cilicia. John addresses the seven churches of Asia. Never is a church acknowledged that stands between the Church universal and the church local.

All will recognise the frailty of human nature and how this may affect a local church. To some it might appear that things would be better if the churches surrendered their authority to a more spiritual and educated body! But as soon as such a surrender is made—to Synod or Council or Assembly or Bishop or Pope—the Saviour is deprived of his crown rights and unseated from his throne. That moment the local church has ceased to be a New Testament church, however expedient its action may appear. That moment the authority of God's Word has been denied.

*Chapter* 3

# THE CHURCH MEETING
# AND MEMBERSHIP

THE Church Meeting is the most characteristic of Congregational institutions. Those of the past dealt with business but in a context which made the concerns of the King of kings preeminent. Necessary, mundane details took a secondary place. There was much praying and Bible reading and preaching. Often there was a faithful dealing with the faults and failings of fellow-members. Warning and entreaty and discipline were seen as an essential part of true fellowship.

Albert Peel quoted Dr Dale as saying, 'To be at a church meeting is for me one of the chief means of grace. To know that I am surrounded by men and women who dwell in God, who have received the Holy Ghost, with whom I am to share the eternal righteousness and eternal rapture of the great life to come, this is blessedness, I breathe a Divine air.'

But how easy it is for a Church Meeting to fall away from this high standard. A clue to that decline is found in a little sentence in a pamphlet on Church Membership published by the former Congregational Union of England and Wales, 'Our system of Church government is democratic'. *Nothing could be further from the truth.* In the Biblical study which was taken from Dale's *Manual* one peak of doctrine towers above the surrounding hillocks. At all costs the authority of Jesus Christ as Supreme Head of his church must be maintained. The problem of the modern Church Meeting is that all too often a Democratic notion has been substituted for a Theocratic principle. The rule of men is substituted for the rule of God.

The finest statement of Congregationalism is provided by the Savoy Declaration. It makes plain the nature of a true gospel church in thirty concise and comprehensive propositions. A satisfactory consideration of the Church Meeting will be greatly helped by summarising a few of the arguments of the Declaration.

1 Church members are properly those whom the Lord Jesus has 'called out of the world unto communion with himself'.
2 A church, then, consists of those who have been gathered by the preaching of the gospel.
3 These 'saints by calling', known to each other by their confession of the faith wrought in them by the power of God, do willingly consent to walk together according to the appointment of Christ giving up themselves to the Lord and to one another by the will of God in professed subjection to the ordinance of the Gospel.
4 Church officers (pastors, teachers, elders and deacons) are chosen and set apart by the church for their work.
5 Admission to the church (and excommunication, or lesser discipline), is to be by the whole church and none are to be admitted to the privileges of the church without 'submission to the rule of Christ in the censures for the government of them'.

# On Joining a Congregational Church

Before more is said about the Church Meeting it is well to consider how it can be ensured that applicants for church membership are, as far as can be ascertained, Christians. No Congregational Church will for long preserve its spiritual life and vitality unless members are accepted with care. This has always presented difficulties. Even when persecution makes Christian commitment hazardous there could be those added in the succession of the status-seeking Simon the Magician who 'believed and was baptised' yet was 'full of bitterness and captive to sin' (Acts 8:9–24).

It is obviously an important function of the pastor and elders to advise the church as to the suitability of a candidate. In some churches, the pastor's recommendation alone is considered sufficient. In most, this would be supported by the testimony of others. The church may appoint one or two members to visit the candidate so that they can add their testimony to the minister's recommendation.

The prospective member's own testimony to his spiritual experience can be a great encouragement to the church and it is good if this can be given by those who visited him, but preferably by the candidate himself, either in public worship or at a weeknight meeting. Some flexibility is desirable, otherwise true but diffident believers may be excluded from the church simply because of their natural weakness. But speech is as natural as breath, and the occasion of giving public testimony to conversion may be the time when the barrier of inhibition is broken down and liberty obtained for wider usefulness and effective Christian service. How greatly, too, such costly witness may be used to the conversion of further souls!

In any church there will be problems which arise because of immature Christians, new converts and awkward sheep. But no church should ever impose conditions which turn it into a private club. The New Testament is plain. All believers are members of the Body of Christ, of the Church. A local church is bound, therefore, to accept as members all those who are Christ's redeemed people. The obligations of the new covenant relationship will be explained. If they are willing to 'submit to the rule of Christ' in the fellowship of his people the church dare not refuse them. They are required by the Lord to enter his church and submit to his authority within it. The church is required to receive them and apply Christ's authority to them.

## The Church Meeting

The object of a Church Meeting should be to seek and to find the Lord in prayer, to hear his Word and receive his marching orders for advance. He promised that where two or three were met in his name, he would be present. If the Lord were indeed present in power at a Church Meeting, would there ever be any of the bickering arguments and self-assertive displays of the natural man which have sometimes shamed God's people? Would they not rather fall at his feet in repentance as Peter prostrated himself in the presence of the risen Saviour? Such an attitude would lead to the recording of more minutes like the following from a Congregational Church Meeting of 1880:

> The whole of the discussion—amidst considerable diversity of sentiment and great warmth of feeling was marked by that united loyalty to the great Head of the Church which desires that he should himself be the ruler of his people.

The Church Meeting should be approached with awe and reverence as well as in loving expectancy. It is not an opportunity to express opinions but to receive orders. The nature of the meeting is such that worship is vital. Testimony to grace needed and given is as appropriate and desirable as in the old-fashioned

Methodist Class-meeting. It hardly needs to be said that the discussions of a Church Meeting are confidential to the members.

The concept of a mere 'business meeting' would hardly withstand the impact of a service of true worship and devotion, praise and testimony. It is a family occasion. Warning and entreaty can be given in love where the public profession of members is thought to fall short of what glorifies God. The young in years and spiritual experience are as free to share as those who are aged and of long experience in the life of Christ.

Those who believe that the gifts of the Holy Spirit are intended for our generation as well as for the apostolic age will look for the exercise of such gifts. Since he distributes 'severally as he wills', the gifts may be manifest through any member. Those who do not accept the continuance of the charismata cannot deny the Scriptural principle of the 'priesthood of all believers'. The Church Meeting is peculiarly appropriate for the ministry of all God's people. Here those who have covenanted together to serve the Lord in fellowship with one another meet for their mutual profit. A long business agenda or infrequency of meeting undermines the purpose of the Church Meeting.

Congregationalists recognise the 'mixed' nature of the meeting. Some members are walking closely with God. The spiritual life of others has waned. The spiritually mature and the 'babe in Christ' are meeting together. All ages are represented and the generation gap of secular society may invade the church. It is evident that these circumstances demand respect for the authority which has been vested in the leaders of the congregation by the Lord, and accepted through the willing suffrage of his people. Whatever form the Church Meeting may take it is always the desire of Congregationalists to be able to say at the close:

It seemed good to the Holy Ghost and to us (Acts 15:28).

# Mutual Concern

Each local church is independent and is fully competent to order its own affairs without external interference and control but it is not intended to be in isolation from other gospel churches.

The Savoy Declaration is most insistent on the responsibility of mutual concern,

> All churches are bound to pray continually for the good or prosperity of all the churches of Christ in all places, and upon all occasions to further it. So the churches themselves (when planted by the providence of God, so as they may have opportunity and advantage of it) ought to hold communion amongst themselves for their peace, increase of love, and mutual edification.

There follows a statement that synods or councils should meet to consider matters of concern, 'in cases of difficulties or differences', and to report back to the churches. This was to be done by the messengers of the local churches. But no authority was committed to such a council.

The 'Objects' of an Evangelical Fellowship of Congregational Churches well express the principle of mutual aid without interference which has characterised Congregationalism through the centuries (see Appendix). Especially has it been true that missionary endeavour at home and abroad has drawn the Congregational churches together in co-operative activity. It is a feeble and apostate Christianity which ignores the cry of the perishing. Today there are many villages in Britain deprived of a faithful gospel testimony. Many populous areas, great housing estates and large industrial towns, are evangelical deserts. The Irish Republic is a mission-field on our doorstep and 'English is spoken'. There are needs that call for mutual association that we may obey Christ's command to take the Gospel 'to every creature'.

Isolation, to a small congregation, so often spells discouragement and despair. Isolation, to a flourishing cause, easily leads to complacency and self-interest. Fellowship brings the blessing of enlarged vision, deepened concern, enriched spiritual experience and an increase in intelligent prayer. Revival fire in one place kindles fire in another.

# And Wider

The old Congregationalists were sure that only their church order was legitimate in the light of Scripture but that did not make them narrow in outlook or limited in association. More than any denomination they abhorred denominationalism. They joined whole-heartedly with those from whom they differed on non-essentials. They were truly catholic in their regard for all the faithful. As early as 1658 they were adamant that 'churches ought not to refuse the communion of each other though they walk not in all things according to the same rules of church order'. They accepted unhesitatingly their fellow believers, however wrong they may have judged their opinions on church government to be. Their belief that 'church' could only mean either a local congregation or the whole body of Christ preserved them from the narrowness and intolerance that would unchurch the saints of another persuasion.

*Chapter* 4

# THE MINISTRY IN
# CONGREGATIONAL CHURCHES

THE Savoy Declaration asserts that the 'officers appointed by Christ to be continued to the end of the world, are pastors, teachers, elders and deacons'.

The world has not yet ended (!) but the separate office of Teacher (as distinct from those known as 'Sunday School Teachers') is virtually unknown today in Congregational Churches. It was not always so. At the end of the sixteenth century the congregation of exiles in Amsterdam enjoyed the ministry of Francis Johnson as Pastor and Henry Ainsworth as Teacher.

The work of pastor and preacher is not strictly that of teacher. True, both pastor and preacher will teach in private and in public as they minister but that is not their special task. The function of the teacher is to instruct and he may serve in a local church or more widely. Perhaps the time will come when a due recognition of Ephesians 4:11 will lead to the restoration of an office lost to Congregationalism. In present practice, the Pastor is often Pastor/Preacher/Teacher.

The titles we give to our church officers are misleading. A deacon is really one who ministers or serves. A minister is really a 'pastor' or 'shepherd', a 'presiding elder', a 'bishop/presbyter' in the local church.

In the New Testament the terms 'elder' and 'bishop' (overseer) are interchangeable. There can be no doubt about this. Ephesians 4:11 refers to 'pastors and teachers' but not to elders or bishops. It seems clear that Paul is using an alternative description of these leaders in Ephesians, one which emphasises their work rather than their status. This is supported by the injunction to elders 'to pastor the flock' (1 Peter 5:2). The reference in Acts 20:28 is, likewise, to the Ephesian elders as 'shepherds' or 'pastors'. When Paul and Barnabas appointed 'elders' or 'presbyters' in the churches which they had founded on their first missionary journey they were appointing shepherds to care for the flock.

The supreme function of elders is the rule of the church. In 1 Timothy 5:17 Paul refers to the elders who rule well as worthy of double honour, especially those who labour in the word and teaching. 1 Thessalonians 5:12 requires respect for those 'Who are over you in the Lord and admonish you'. Hebrews 13:17 is stronger: 'Obey them that have the rule over you and submit to them'. The reason is that 'they are keeping watch over your souls, as men who will have to give account'.

It should be apparent that godly rule must be in accordance with the Scriptures. There is a profound difference between the subservience of the cults to their leaders and the free obedience of the people of God. Christian obedience is to the Lord who has appointed his servants to minister in this respect. Their 'rule' is so to admonish that the church conforms to the pattern of the Word in doctrine and conduct. This makes them inevitably teachers of that Word and expositors of its application to the flock. It is arguable that there were elders who were not teachers. Such inference is drawn from the qualifying phrase of 1 Timothy 5:17 'especially those who labour in the Word and in teaching'. The condition that a bishop should be an 'apt teacher' (1 Timothy 3:2), 'able to give instruction in sound doctrine and also to confute those who contradict it' (Titus 1:9), suggests that it must be rare to appoint as elder a man who lacks such qualification.

## Godly Discipline

There will always be problems associated with pastoral oversight. To admonish lovingly and to correct graciously can only be done in the love of Christ. Some judgments are hard to make and discipline not readily administered. Authority can soon be debased into authoritarianism and discipline decline into self-assertiveness. Underlying the pastoral office is the supposition that its holder has been humbled by grace and lives in conscious and deliberate submission to the Scripture of truth. Spiritual maturity implies loving and sympathetic identification with the wayward rather than the superiority of the 'knowledge that puffs up.

Equally, it is hard for the heart of man to accept meekly God's word of reproof from the lips of a fellow sinner. It is not easy even when it is manifest that the reprover is a mouthpiece of God by the evidence of a holy and sacrificial life and the favour of God upon him. Resistance to correction and resentment at rebuke are typical of unspirituality. Who would be bold to deny that the general condition of the church of our times shows every evidence of experiencing God's judgment? Compared with the vital effectiveness of the church in other lands we are in a parlous state. Decade after decade passes without a true spiritual awakening. When the fallacy that a church is a 'democracy' is accepted this can only aggravate the modern tendency to rebel against authority and truth. The refrain that comments on the days of the Judges could likewise spell the obituary notice of many a congregation of our times. 'There was no king in Israel, every man did what was right in his own eyes.'

It is difficult to exercise Scriptural discipline in an age of indiscipline and spiritual poverty. It is doubly difficult when the task falls to the lot of one man. A small church may have no one of spiritual calibre adequate to share the responsibility of godly rule with the minister. Where there are those of such calibre there needs to be a speedy return to the Congregational practice of a plurality of elders to care for the flock, as was the practice of the apostolic age.

## The Status of a Minister

Too many churches have experienced ministry at the hands of ordained men lacking a true gospel faith. This has led to some suspicion of the pastorate. The mischief of an unconverted ministry is not only the evils done to a particular congregation at the time: it is also the disrepute into which the ministry may fall in the common regard of God's people. Of course it is wrong for men unsound in the faith and lacking the divine commission to be elected and called to the pastorate. The enemy of souls will make every effort to secure their acceptance by the churches of the redeemed. This, however, does not excuse the failure of congregations to accept the shepherdly guidance of those whose ordination was first by the nail-pierced hands of the Redeemer and only secondly by a local church.

When a church calls a minister to be its pastor it has done so after spending much time in prayer and in consideration of the spiritual and practical qualifications of the man concerned. They will appreciate the value of a man of learning for he should be 'a good minister of Jesus Christ, nourished up in the words of faith and of good doctrine' (1 Timothy 4:6), but they will not despise a man of no academic training, for they will recall that the apostles Peter and John, though regarded as 'unlearned and ignorant men' were yet heeded as those who 'had been with Jesus'. A church might receive more blessing through one who had spent much time with Jesus than one who had read many books about him. Though obviously a combination of the two could be an improvement on either.

Another Scriptural qualification would be the fruitfulness of a man's previous service for the Lord. According to the apostle Paul, this is a better commendation than any written certificate (2 Corinthians 3:1–3). So Timothy was bidden to 'lay hands suddenly on no man' (1 Timothy 5:22). So Titus was urged to exercise care in the appointment of elders:

> Since an overseer is entrusted with God's work, he must be blameless—not overbearing, not quick-tempered, not given to much wine, not violent, not pursuing dishonest gain. Rather he must be hospitable, one who loves what is good, who is self-controlled, upright, holy and disciplined. He must hold firmly to the trustworthy message as it has been taught, so that he can encourage others by sound doctrine and refute those who oppose it (Titus 1:7–9 NIV).

Ordination in a Congregational Church is a recognition that the Lord Jesus Christ, the only Head of the Church, has already called out and set apart a man for the ministry. The church recognises God's grace and the gifts of his Spirit and publicly acknowledges that a man is separated to the Lord's service. It is the local church that ordains but, by invitation, brethren of other churches usually join with representatives of the local church in laying hands on the ordinand.

## Dismissal of a Pastor

The Savoy Declaration refers to 'The Lord Christ having given to his called ones ... liberty and power to choose persons fitted by the Holy Ghost ... to be over them, and to minister to them in the Lord'. There is no reference, however, to the dismissal of those so called.

The right of dismissal must remain with the Church Meeting for it is the final authority under God for the life of the particular congregation. But such a right should be exercised rarely and with extreme care.

It would be very unwise for a church to consider dismissing a pastor just because they do not like what he has to say to them. It may be that God wants to give that church a message like that of a Jeremiah and sends them just such a prophet. If the church, having previously declared that they had recognised the Lord's call to the ministry and to the pastorate, should then find that they do not relish God's message of warning or exhortation, they would surely seek to be rid of their minister at their peril.

On the other hand, it is a tragedy when a pastor assumes, or is allowed to assume, an exclusive authority over the church's affairs contrary to the teaching of the New Testament. Even with authentic evangelical convictions, a man of high principle may alienate a congregation or so fail in certain marks of his character that he presides over a church's decline to a point where, apart from special Divine intervention, recovery is virtually impossible.

Early Congregational Trust Deeds stated that a church was free to dismiss a minister who was guilty of immorality, or who had abandoned the doctrines he had undertaken to maintain, or ceased to do the work of pastor to which he had been called.

Obviously, no minister is entitled to insist on believers' baptism only in a church that has a paedo-baptist foundation. Nor may he preach Arminianism in a church that has Calvinistic doctrines written into its Trust Deed. Modern Trust Deeds generally allow great latitude in doctrines, requiring only that they be 'according to the principles and usages for the time being held by the congregational denomination'. Most older Deeds, however, require very definite doctrines to be held and taught. If a minister fails to do so he can properly be dismissed by the church.

Finally, it should be noted that a church does not employ a minister. It releases him from the need of secular employment and undertakes properly to maintain him and his family so that he may do the Lord's work among them. He is not a servant of the church but of the Lord who directs his work and who may give him a vocation wider than the narrow interest of a particular congregation. Where there is mutual love in Christ, there will be mutual understanding and support.

## The Office of Deacon

When we turn to the office of deacons we have moved into a very different category of ministry, though the identification of the offices of elder and deacon is a long-standing Congregational tradition. The 'diaconate' is considered to incorporate both elders and deacons. The failure to distinguish between the two has been a cause of much confusion and weakness among our churches. There has also often been a misunderstanding of the need for the spiritual status of the deacon. In Acts 6 we read that

the twelve summoned the body of the disciples and said: 'It is not right that we should give up preaching the word of God to serve tables. Therefore, brethren, pick out from among you seven men of good repute, full of the Spirit and of wisdom, whom we may

appoint to this duty. But we will devote ourselves to prayer and
to the ministry of the word.'

We should notice the qualifications of these men, the nature of
their work and the distinction between their ministry and that
of the apostles.

First, they were to be men of good reputation among their
fellow-believers, Spirit-filled men and wise men. The modern
deacon may gain office because of his practical wisdom in matters
of business. He may be skilful with figures or capable in dealing
with the church buildings. Such gifts are welcome, but he may
not be recognised as one of the most spiritually-minded among
the brethren. Bezaleel, in Exodus 31, worked in metal and wood
and fabric for the Tabernacle but, because it was for the service
of God, he needed to be a man filled with God's Holy Spirit.
No less under the new covenant! A deacon was to be no novice.
Let them be 'tested first, then if they prove themselves blameless
let them serve as deacons' (1 Timothy 3:10). To 'serve tables'
deacons must still be men of prayer as ready to receive direction
from God as they grapple with a leaky roof as the elders must
be when tackling a leaky tongue.

Secondly, the work of a deacon is described as 'serving tables'.
The context shows they were to be occupied with the relief of
material needs in the New Testament church. The importance
of such work is obscured by the affluence of our society. Need
is still present. It may be the secret penury of a Christian wife
whose unconverted husband deprives her of the very necessities
of life. The work of a deacon may be to assist an elderly member
through the intricate maze of the social services and their
regulations. Deacons were responsible to the church for the care
of the sick and the widows and the orphans. They relieved others
of responsibility in the realm of the practical. At the time there
were no buildings with which to be bothered. The basic principle

is unchanged. The apostles were to be set free from concern over such matters.

Thirdly, there is a distinction drawn between this service and the ministry of prayer and preaching which was the supreme preoccupation of the apostles. Yet the deacons were not precluded from prayer and preaching. The longest sermon-outline in Acts follows immediately upon the appointment of the first deacons. It is a message proclaimed by the deacon, Stephen. But deacons need not be preachers or teachers. Theirs is a secondary office but it is one that demands spirituality for its exercise. It should set pastors and elders free from involvement in the practical affairs that are inseparable from the life of the Christian community.

We could stop at this point. We are considering the ministry in Congregational Churches. There are pastors and teachers, often combined in one person. All pastors are elders and, in one sense, all elders are pastors. There are also deacons. Beyond this lies the whole realm of the priesthood of all believers which Congregationalists have frequently neglected to the detriment of their spiritual life and to the reduction of their effectiveness in witness.

The church at Jerusalem, outlined at the end of Acts 2, presents a picture far removed from the institutionalism that developed over the years and perhaps reached its climax in the late 19th century where a church might consist of all sorts of organisations and bodies often operating on their own. Early Congregationalists sought to recapture the community life of the church—a big and friendly family in a neighbourhood, often in each other's homes, conversing over the things of God, and praying together.

*Chapter 5*

# THE CONFESSIONS OF CONGREGATIONALISM

THE apostle John, notwithstanding all his emphasis upon love, wrote in his third epistle, 'I have no greater joy than to hear that my children are living according to the truth'. Theology is a forbidding word, and doctrine not much better, nevertheless they are the means by which we set out the truths of our faith. Congregationalists have always been prepared to set out such truths and held a consistent position on Evangelical doctrine throughout their history until the drift into the apostasy of the last few generations.

That drift can be seen in the alterations made to the Constitution of the Congregational Union of England and Wales over this period. Until 1904 the first two Objects of the Union were:

1  To uphold and extend Evangelical religion primarily in connexion with churches of the Congregational order.
2  To promote Scriptural views of Church fellowship and organisation.

In 1904, these were changed to:

1 To extend and realise the Kingdom of Christ, primarily through Churches of the Congregational Order.
2 To promote New Testament principles of Church fellowship and organisation.

In 1958, much greater changes were made to:

1 To serve and bear witness to the Kingdom of God by confessing and proclaiming Almighty God as Creator, Sustainer and Father of all, Jesus Christ his Son as Lord and Saviour, and the Holy Spirit as the living power of God.
2 To promote principles of church fellowship and organisation that are consonant with the Gospel.

It will be noted that, first, 'Evangelical' disappears, then 'Congregational', and also 'Scriptural' or 'New Testament'. The credal statement in 1958 is extremely vague with the Holy Spirit not even warranting capital letters as the 'Living Power' of God.

Historian Albert Peel (in his book *These Hundred Years*) wrote of the stirring of opposition to Biblical authority and the truths of Evangelical religion in the 1870s and recorded a resolution debated and carried by an overwhelming majority by the Assembly of the Congregational Union of England and Wales in 1878.

That in view of the uneasiness produced in the churches of the congregational order by the proceedings of the recent Conference at Leicester on the terms of Religious Communion, the Assembly feels called upon to reaffirm that the primary object of the Congregational Union is, according to the terms of its own constitution, to uphold and extend Evangelical religion. That the Assembly appeals to the history of Congregational churches generally, as evidence that Congregationalists have always regarded the acceptance of the Facts and Doctrines of the Evangelical Faith revealed in the Holy Scriptures of the Old and New Testaments as an essential condition of Religious Communion in Congregational Churches: and that among these have always been included the Incarnation, the Atoning Sacrifice of the Lord Jesus Christ, his

Resurrection, his Ascension and Mediatorial Reign, and the work of the Holy Spirit in the renewal of men. That the Congregational Union was established on the Basis of these Facts and Doctrines is, on the judgment of the Assembly, made evident by the Declaration of Faith and Order adopted at the Annual Meeting 1833: and that the Assembly believes that the churches represented in the Union hold these Facts and Doctrines in their integrity to this day.

It is, therefore, a modern myth that Congregationalism rejects all creeds. This myth suggests that it requires no doctrinal position to be held by its members. It exalts liberty of conscience and freedom of thought above all else, especially above doctrinal conformity.

In the series of Congregational Union pamphlets already mentioned, one writer refers to the requirements for Church Membership in this way:

> We know that in our theological interpretations we are bound to differ. Nor do we ask whether you have passed through a certain emotional experience. Our question goes deeper than theology and deeper than emotion. It goes right down to the centre. We ask: 'Are you wanting to be like Christ?' If we might put it more simply still: 'Are you in earnest about being good?'

If such ideas were true this present chapter would be pointless. There would be no reason to question prospective church members about their beliefs or their experience of new birth in Christ. There would be no place for a 'Basis of Faith' of the Evangelical Fellowship of Congregational Churches in one of the Appendices at the end of this book. There would have been no statements of faith throughout the past four hundred years of Congregational history.

# No Imposition of Creeds

There is, however, a faint glimmer of reason in the anti-creed myth. Congregationalism has steadfastly repudiated the imposition of creeds. In a preamble to the Savoy Declaration we read:

> Whatever is of force or constraint in matters of this nature causeth them to degenerate from the name and nature of confessions: and turns them from being Confessions of Faith, into exactions and impositions of Faith.

No one can be made a Christian by mental assent to truth. But, having become a Christian, he will know what he believes and will be able to say to a fellow-Christian:

> Here are truths that we hold in common: let us declare them together in the fellowship of the Church.

Congregationalists have never demanded assent to a creed. They have declared their faith in a 'Confession'. These declarations have been approved by the separate and independent congregations through their representatives. This was so with the Savoy Declaration in 1658. It has also been customary for the various congregations to incorporate a statement of doctrines in their Trust Deed. The earliest statement extant was by a particular congregation in 1596. It was a defence for a church which had been suffering persecution, made jointly on behalf of those who *were exiles* in Amsterdam and their fellow-believers who remained in London. It was described as *'A True Confession of the Faith (of those) falsely called Brownists—published for the clearing of ourselves from slanders of heresy, schism, disloyalty, sedition given out against us'.*

When the delegates of 120 Congregational Churches met in 1658 they appointed a committee of six to draw up a Declaration. In due course this 'was agreed upon and consented unto by their Elders and Messengers in their Meeting at the Savoy'. When the Congregational Union adopted its 'Declaration of the Faith, Church Order and Discipline of the Congregational or Independent Dissenters' in 1833 it is significant that it repeated the traditional Congregational objection to the usefulness of creeds. Yet in the same breath they claimed to be: 'far more agreed in their doctrines and practices than any Church which enjoins subscription and enforces a human standard of orthodoxy: and they believe that there is no minister and no church among them that would deny the substance of any one of the following doctrines of religion, though each might prefer to state his sentiments in his own way'.

Finally, we refer to the 'Basis of Faith' of EFCC, drawn up in 1967. In the Fellowship's Constitution there is stated: 'In order that the witness of the associated churches may be clear a Statement of Scriptural principles has been drawn up to act as a 'BASIS OF FELLOWSHIP'. This is not a creed we seek to impose upon others, but a testimony to what we ourselves believe. The foundation of the whole Basis is an acceptance of the Divine inspiration and supreme authority of the Bible, and if any statement therein can be shown to be unscriptural it will be corrected at once.'

## Evangelical and Reformed

What then are these foundational truths which are considered to belong to true Congregationalism whether we talk of 1596, 1658, 1833 or 1967? First and foremost, they were and are held to be Scriptural. Two other words would be adequate as summary. The confessions are 'EVANGELICAL' and 'REFORMED'. Unfortunately neither word has a clear meaning today. 'Evangelical' can be misunderstood to mean no more than 'evangelistic'—a general commitment to the idea of outreach. It can be so broad as to signify no more than a vague dependency on grace for salvation rather than upon 'works' or upon 'church' or 'sacraments'. It is usually used by the media to mean 'charismatic'. 'Reformed' can mean, as in the title 'United Reformed Church', little more than a claim to historical succession from the Reformers of an earlier age.

The 'Evangelical and Reformed' faith cannot be separated from its absolute dependence upon a divinely inspired and infallible Bible as the sole authority for the teaching and practice of the Church. When the Reformers rejected the authority of Pope and priest, they did so only because they were led to see that a higher authority existed upon which alone the Church was established by Christ and by which alone it could be continued in obedience to him.

Thus the first chapter of the Savoy Declaration is entitled 'Of the Holy Scriptures': thus the 1833 Declaration begins: 'The Scriptures of the Old Testament, as received from the Jews, and the books of the New Testament, as received by the Primitive Christians from the Evangelists and Apostles, Congregational Churches believe to be Divinely inspired, and of supreme authority': thus the first statement of EFCC Basis of Faith declares: 'THE WRITTEN WORD: God's greatness and holiness are such that, without his aid, man can neither understand God nor find the way to a right relationship with him. In his mercy, however, God has made himself known. He has done this, partially, through Creation, but explicitly through the Old and New Testaments of the Bible. We therefore accept all that was written in the Bible as not merely containing, but being, the inspired and infallible Word of God and the final and sufficient authority in all matters of Christian faith and life.'

As the whole EFCC Basis of Faith is set out later as an Appendix it is unnecessary to do more than draw attention to it. It is modern and concise. Compared with the 32 chapters and more of the 'Savoy', it is very brief. The two longest paragraphs deal with the Bible and with the Lord Jesus Christ as God and Saviour. The phrase 'all that was written in the Bible as not merely containing, but being, the inspired and infallible Word of God' makes obvious reference to the current issue in the church known as 'neo-orthodoxy' or 'neo-Calvinism' in which the Bible may be appealed to as a source of truth without the necessity of accepting it as a whole. Emphasis is laid on 'Substitution' in the choice of words that describe the atonement.

It may be claimed that a brief statement was sufficient to align EFCC with other contemporary evangelical societies or associations but the blurring of the lines of demarcation since 1967 has proceeded at such a pace that doubt may be raised on this point. However, it is claimed that the Basis stands in true succession to the earlier Confessions and may be read in their light.

By comparison the Savoy Declaration seems to attempt to summarise a whole library of theology. It has few differences from the earlier Westminster Confession approved by Parliament in 1642. In some paragraphs there are minor verbal changes. The Savoy omits a few clauses.

It should be remembered that both the Westminster and the Savoy belong to the period of the Commonwealth and that behind both lie the Anglican 'Articles of Religion'. The burning issues of Conformity and State relationship, of the laws of the land in the light of the laws of God, demanded treatment in a 17th century Confession whereas present-day evangelicals would regard a definition of the Scriptural teaching on such topics as Sabbath Observance, the Civil Magistrate, and Marriage as unnecessary in a Statement of Faith.

The other great debate of the 17th century was the controversy associated with the name of Arminius. Arminian teaching lays stress upon the part that man plays in the work of his salvation. The strong emphasis on 'predestination' in the Savoy and its thorough exposition of 'grace' stems from this debate. These doctrines had been firmly expounded by John Calvin. Historically, Congregational Churches have been clearly and positively Calvinistic though the intensity with which they have maintained 'Reformed' doctrine has varied. Within that theological tradition they have suffered the barrenness that results from a dead orthodoxy, and also they have known the glorious vitality that flows from a full and explicit dependence upon God, who in grace and by his Spirit quickens the dead and revives his Church.

Our present age is humanistic in its thinking and, as humanism is diametrically opposed to a God-centred, God-dependent faith, our thinking is likely to be so conditioned that we find the theology of the Puritans uncongenial. If, on the other hand, we are determined to submit to the Word of God we shall find the robust statements of the Savoy Declaration meet our need. Here is a clear exposition of the Scriptures in matters essential to the life and work of the Church as well as the life of the individual.

A belief that God has chosen his elect in Christ from the foundation of the world should not weaken but rather enthuse evangelistic endeavour. The preacher is encouraged to unshakeable confidence that God can turn the hearts of the most wayward to him. George Whitefield is a supreme example of a man who had no doubt of man's inability to respond to the Gospel apart from grace. Yet his preaching, and that of so many who believed as he did, was with fire and with tears. There was no fatalism about their attitude to the perishing. The sovereignty of God was a comfort to their hearts and a sure ground for confidence as they prayed and as they preached.

Space does not allow the expounding of the Savoy Declaration in any detail. Readers should study it, Bible in hand. The writers thought of man as a fallen creature whose will had been brought into bondage through sin. That is not mere orthodoxy: it is a salutary reminder of our true nature. How greatly such a truth is needed when a counterfeit gospel is so widespread—the political/ social counterfeit which is the religious stance typified by the World Council of Churches. The Declaration accepts the state of man as corrupt but it exalts Christ as the sinless Saviour and all-sufficient Redeemer of lost mankind. It acknowledges that we suffer the effects of depravity in every aspect of our being but it declares that in Christ God became man. Christ's eternal Godhead, his human and divine natures, his intercession and his personal return are spelt out in positive terms of unmistakeable clarity.

## Is 'Congregationalism' Simply Church Order?

It may be argued that 'Congregational' is a word that should be applied only to the doctrine of the Church. Technically, that could be admitted, but to divorce Congregationalism from its history and theological tradition is to deny the mainspring of its effectiveness. Godly men became Congregational Independents because they believed the Bible to be God's Word, because they held the great reformed doctrines, the faith expressed in their Confessions. Because of their beliefs and spiritual experience they 'suffered mocking and scourging, even chains and imprisonment'. Through faith they 'conquered kingdoms, enforced justice, became mighty in war, put foreign armies to flight'. It was because of this faith that churches were planted until their number in England and Wales approached five thousand. With the waning of that faith, this century has seen the decline of that work. Those who denied the truth of God were denied the power of God. Miracles of grace ceased, churches closed. Ultimately, with the setting up of the Congregational Church in England and Wales, followed so soon by the formation of the United Reformed Church, there came the denial of the Independent churchmanship that was one of Congregationalism's chief glories.

It is not only the church order but also the faith of our forefathers that we need to cherish and propagate. They held that faith, not in a vacuum, but in the context of a fervent zeal. So through trials and tribulations God was with them and prospered their endeavours. Not just the same churchmanship, but the same faith, and the same spirituality, are needed if we, their successors, are to experience God's hand upon us for good.

*Chapter 6*

# WORSHIP IN CONGREGATIONAL CHURCHES

THE early Independents took a very poor view of liturgical worship and spoke pungently, even harshly, of 'praying with a book'. The resurgence of set forms of prayer and the extensive use of liturgy is often excused today as helping to involve the congregation more fully in worship. It is more likely to derive from a lack of spiritual fife in pulpit and pew. Set forms can be used as an attempt to conceal the barrenness of the devotional land.

The form of worship which is part and parcel of Congregationalism is more demanding of the worshipper than any other, just as its Scriptural order of church government demands more of the members than other systems. It demands spirituality.

The major elements in worship are praise, prayer and preaching. There is a common practice of reading some verses from the Bible as a 'call to worship'. This can be useful. It can be significant as God directs his people to seek him. The Bible readings are most commonly related to the subject matter of the sermon that will come later. Such reading can be accompanied by explanatory comments and thus serve the purpose of helping in the instruction of the congregation. This analysis of a service places the Bible reading within the general category of the preaching.

The worship of Congregational Churches has traditionally been marked by a serious reverence and simple joy. The cheery familiarities of some modern gospel rallies would seem strange and indecorous to our forefathers. The liveliness of a service did not depend on artificial aids. If life did not come with the worshippers as they entered God's house to meet with him, or come with the preacher as he left God's presence with the burden of his message on his heart it could not be manufactured. There was to be no 'false fire'. Their buildings were known as 'Meeting Houses'. The worshippers came to meet with one another. And to meet with God as well.

## Hymns and Spiritual Songs

The praise of the whole Church of God was transformed by the contribution of Isaac Watts to hymnody. One day at home he complained of the poetic standard of the metrical psalms and the few hymns sung at church each Lord's Day. He was challenged to do better. He did! Watts' *Psalms and Hymns* became the vehicle for expressing the praises of Congregational Churches for more than a century. Every worthwhile hymn book, down to the very latest to be published, contains a good selection of his verse.

One of Watts' great merits was that he wrote good poetry, with the restraint on language and imagery that hymns demand. There are some, to us, quaint expressions. There is a sprinkling of uncharacteristic doggerel. More than this, however, he released worship from bondage to the psalter, and his paraphrases elevated the psalms from the level of the Old Testament to that of the New. Most important, his hymns express sound Scriptural truth and deep devotional feeling. How many of our very greatest hymns came from the pen of Isaac Watts! 'When I survey the wondrous Cross' is surely among the very finest, if not the finest, in the English language.

Churches which do not recite a Creed or repeat a 'General Thanksgiving' or a 'General Confession' need nonetheless to incorporate such aspects of worship into the service. This makes hymn singing so important. Adoration and praise are essential. Assurance and testimony are appropriate whenever we meet. Is this not indication enough that no believer is excluded from participation in a service even if his voice be no better than a raven's croak? To conduct a service with a congregation that sings as if they mean every word is an exhilarating experience. How easy then to pray publicly and preach earnestly!

There is a contemporary relevance to all this. Although language changes, and Watts and Doddridge may sometimes sound strange to the ears of modern man, yet the great truths expressed in these older hymns are still capable of touching and enriching the mental and emotional life of a 20th century congregation. The rich vocabulary of Watts or Wesley may puzzle some, but their hymns are to be preferred to the sentimental ballads of the Victorian era; and many doctrinally weak, and often poorly written, contemporary hymns. With occasional brief explanations from the Minister, younger Christians will soon come to appreciate, and delight in the hymns of Watts, Wesley, Doddridge, Newton and Cowper, and see them as, not only a means of enriching their faith, but as guides to a deeper and more profound knowledge of God.

# Praying and Preaching

Public prayer is a topic that presents many Christians with difficulty. Some argue that the leading of prayer in worship should not be restricted to the preacher alone. True, it is not desirable that his should be the only voice raised in every service. On the other hand, public prayer must be audible or the congregation cannot enter into the petitions. A standard of dignity in language needs to be maintained, a standard below which free prayer is liable to fall. The pastor-preacher knows what is to come as the service continues, he is aware of the particular needs within the congregation and has taken thought over the matters in church and state which should occupy the minds of the congregation. As they are led in prayer the people must be deeply concerned to join in what is said on their behalf. They must want to confess their sins, rejoice in forgiveness, plead for the lost and cry to God for revival. Their hearts must be warmed by the thought of the riches of their spiritual inheritance in Christ and they must feel for their persecuted brethren in other lands. If they do not 'pray in their prayers' as did Elijah (James 5:17), a deadness will creep over the whole service. If they follow closely and enter fully into the praying, the 'long prayer' of our tradition will seem all too short. It will be a most precious and blessed part of the service.

Older Independent churches all had central pulpits. This emphasised the centrality of the Word and they were designed so that every member of the congregation would be able to hear the word preached. The preaching was the culmination of worship. All that went before had been leading up to the moment when God spoke to his people by the mouth of his servant. It was not time for a few random thoughts or a sermonette. It was an occasion for the thorough, scholarly (and often lengthy) exposition of the passage under consideration. Whatever their verbosity, the old preachers were seldom guilty of superficiality in their proclamation of God's Word. It was a sign of decadence when congregations gathered to admire the rhetorical fireworks of a pulpiteer, laugh at his humorous anecdotes, or notice his political allusions.

Teaching is not the essence of this part of the service though much will be learnt. Preaching is aimed at the will through the mind and the emotions. If it is truly prophetic it will demand a verdict. Preaching is intended to proclaim the truth of God through his Word, in the power of God's Spirit and in the name of the Lord. A verdict should be demanded on the basis of truth presented, truth not given coldly but with passion. The response may be of repentance and faith. It may be thankfulness and praise. It may be obedience to the call to service. Some unpremeditated aside may have come home to the hearer's conscience fruitfully. The logic of an argument may have convinced the mind and brought response. The fervour and conviction of the preacher may have touched the heart. However God has spoken, it was His grace that moved the true response.

The preaching that is truly in the Congregational tradition will be Biblical and evangelical and serious and demanding. It will involve the whole personality of the preacher as well as his knowledge and training. Above all it will express not just a capacity for fluent speech, even true eloquence, but rather the burning heart, the passion for souls, the vibrant concern for God's will to be done on earth.

The closing hymn ought to provide opportunity for the hearer to express his response to the message preached. He will be saying in song that he has freshly surrendered his will to conform to God's will and purpose.

*Chapter 7*

# THE SACRAMENTS IN CONGREGATIONAL CHURCHES

## The Lord's Supper

THE usual practice of Congregational Churches is to observe the Lord's Supper once or twice a month, generally as a brief addition to morning or evening worship. In some churches a weekly observance as part of the service of praise and preaching is appreciated as valuable. Thus the message of the sacrament becomes a culmination of all that has preceded. The general rule is that those who serve are elders or deacons. The minister or another elder presides. In the pattern of fixed pews (or of the brief remembrance after public worship), no attempt is made to sit around the communion table. By remaining in their seats the participants symbolise the normal posture for a meal. They take bread and wine individually or unitedly according to the custom of the particular church or as directed by the presiding minister. Often those who serve or others in the congregation are asked to lead in prayer. Sometimes open prayer is part of the service either before or after the distribution of the elements.

Variety in the manner of observance does not imply any serious difference of opinion concerning the meaning and significance of the Supper. First and foremost it proclaims the Gospel. The good news of saving grace is set forth visibly as broken bread and poured out wine are displayed and then taken. In the past it was sometimes described as a 'saving ordinance'. The centrality of the Cross is made plain. Whenever this most important Christian rite is celebrated, the way of salvation is shown to be Christ himself, the Way, the Truth and the Life. It acts as a constant corrective to misrepresentations of Christianity. The communion table is a clear denial of any theory that makes religion to be a matter of good works. Such would be a religion with no room for a Cross. Nor can the idea that religion consists only of an intellectual understanding of ultimate truth stand against the Supper. Those whose minds consider the Cross to be foolishness make their presence at Christ's table a mockery, for they face that Cross as the symbol and centre of the Christian religion.

At the same time the Congregational form of the Lord's Supper allows neither priestly function nor superstition to play a part. There is no kneeling as if to worship the elements. There are no priestly words of consecration to convert bread and wine into a different substance, supposedly, the actual body and blood of Christ. Instead there is the simple declaration of the apostle Paul's word to the Corinthians that this act is to be a remembrance of the Saviour and of his redemptive work. That the Lord Jesus is present goes without saying, by his Spirit and his Word—for this is his table, and this is his church.

The service calls disciples to recall the cost of their salvation. This should quicken them to fresh whole-heartedness in commitment to him. It is a time of renewal of covenant relationship to their Lord. It is a solemn service because of all that is implied in a moment of the consecration of themselves.

The oneness of the church is clear at the Table. Here 'earth's distinctions disappear'. Sinners saved by grace alone join together in thankfulness and in acknowledgement of personal worthlessness. A 'closed' table is singularly inappropriate. It is not for us to exclude anyone who has been saved from hell. If Christ has made a saint out of a sinner he should he as welcome at his table as any of those who belong to the membership of a particular local church. The warning that the Supper is for believers only should be sufficiently clear to discourage unbelievers from partaking. They should be more than welcome to remain and watch. This was common in the past. The children of the families of the church would stay with others and gain much profit. If we were attracting more people to hear the Gospel who recognise themselves as outside the Kingdom but have a longing to enter, it would be easier to restore such a practice. May the witness of our churches become speedily effective so that this situation may be reproduced.

## Baptism

Congregational churches baptise converts to Christianity, and also the children of a believing parent. Their theological starting point is the emphasis laid by reformed theology on the grace of God. Baptism (according to the Savoy Declaration) 'is a sacrament of the New Testament, ordained by Jesus Christ to be unto the party baptised a sign and seal of the covenant of grace'.

In baptism, God declares his grace by a 'visual aid'. The convert, a believer, is acknowledging that God, in his mercy, has saved him and that he is submitting to the Lordship of Christ. The believing parents of the infant acknowledge God's graciousness to them and look forward to the fulfilling of his covenant promise in saving their child. The local church, similarly, remembers God's covenant mercy and rejoices in confidence that God will save. 'Dipping of the person into the water is not necessary [again quoting the Savoy Declaration] but baptism is rightly administered by pouring or sprinkling water upon the person.'

Congregationalists hold that the true Church comprises the covenant-people of God. The church is the heir of the covenant promises, just as Israel in the Old Testament was God's covenant people. The Israelite child was circumcised and so recognised as belonging to the covenant-people and to enjoy its privileges and responsibilities. As circumcision was the sign of the old covenant so baptism is the sign of the new. So the child of the Christian home is regarded as an heir to promises and is baptised as a declaration of God's grace and of the Church's trust in God's faithfulness.

Dr Dale argues for the indiscriminate use of the ordinance. His case was based on a narrow reading of Matthew 28:18–20. Christ's authority as the risen Lord was absolute 'over all nations' to make disciples and to baptise. He interprets the vital words thus: 'Go ye, therefore, and make disciples of all the nations, baptising (all the nations) into the name of the Father, and of the Son, and of the Holy Ghost: teaching (all the nations) to observe all things whatsoever I command you.' Thus the command to baptise and to teach are treated as of equal relevance and of universal application. Dale's view has little to commend it Scripturally and is quite a novelty to earlier Congregational thinking.

The opposite extreme, of baptising no infants at all, is equally far removed from Congregational thinking. With hardly a dissident voice Trust Deeds specify that the properties they protect are reserved 'for the use of Protestant Dissenters of the Independent or Congregational denomination, practising paedobaptism', that is, the baptism of infants. The Congregational position is made clear by quoting the relevant paragraph of the Savoy Declaration. 'Not only those that do actually profess faith in and obedience unto Christ. but also the infants of one or both believing parents are to be baptised, and those only.'

The first words should be noted. There is no refusal of the convert requesting baptism. The heathen, whether of the mission field or of pagan Britain, is to be baptised when he confesses Christ as Saviour. Secondly, there is the restriction to the children of believers. This double position is borne out by the 1833 Declaration: 'They believe in the perpetual obligation of Baptism ... to be administered to all converts to Christianity and their children ...'.

The Scriptures show the clear difference and supreme privilege of being brought up within the community of Israel as against belonging to a pagan nation. The Israelite had the Word of God, the ministry of the prophets, priests and kings.

Similarly, the condition of a child nurtured in a Christian home is very different from that of a child brought up in spiritual darkness. The believing parent surrounds his children with prayer and gospel truth. All the promises of the covenant-relationship into which the parents themselves have entered by grace are applicable to their offspring. The reality of these promises can be seen in the Christian homes of the churches. The moment of new birth may be delayed, but any covenant that God himself has made he will keep.

It is accepted that the discussion of Baptism is much to the fore in the present day. As in all things, love must be pre-eminent. Love seeks to understand and sympathise with the standpoint of brethren from whom we differ. Such love can win the response of a similar desire to understand our own emphasis. Paul insisted that love should take priority over knowledge. Such love, in harness with humility, will lead inevitably to the conclusion that we are unlikely to resolve a problem that has defied the most saintly and scholarly of Christians for so many centuries. Such love could even make us less concerned that it should be resolved.

PT Forsyth, perhaps the foremost Congregational theologian of recent times, expressed a conciliatory position which does not renounce long-held attitudes:

> The two forms of Baptism ... and their ministers, should be equally valid at choice in Churches of the same polity, each filling out a hemisphere of the whole truth on that subject, There are questions, I know, of historic tradition, of a separate existence dearly bought, of dear denominational ties which no scheme must despise or override, or treat with anything but respect. But they will all fall into place by consent as the passion and ideal of evangelical unity comes to work like a fire in our bones.

*Chapter* 8

# THE FUTURE FOR
# CONGREGATIONALISM

SOME who will have read thus far may still be concerned that, in these days of much emphasis upon Church Unity, there should be published a work setting out denominational distinctions. To any such, we would quote the words used by RW Dale over 100 years ago in the introduction to his *Manual of Congregational Principles*. They have a familiar ring.

> At a time when Christendom is agitated by controversies reaching to the very roots of the Christian Faith, and when all Churches are struggling with practical duties which are beyond their strength, questions of ecclesiastical polity may appear to have no claim to consideration.

> We have to assert the authority and grace of our Lord Jesus Christ against the assaults of speculative unbelief. We have to preach the Gospel to those who have never heard it. We have to lessen the miseries as well as the sins of mankind. There are hundreds of millions of heathen men to whom the redemption of the world

by Jesus Christ is altogether unknown: there are vast numbers of our own countrymen who have drifted beyond the reach of all the ordinary institutions of Christian instruction and worship: there are the hungry to be fed and the naked to be clothed: there are low conceptions of morality in domestic, commercial, and public life which the Church ought to elevate: there is selfishness in the Church itself which ought to be inspired with the charity of Christ, indolence which ought to be set on fire by the zeal of Christ for the honour of God and the righteousness and happiness of mankind. It may be thought that when these great tasks are done it will be time enough to consider whether Episcopacy, Presbyterianism, or Congregationalism is the best form of church polity.

But, meantime, churches actually exist, and they cannot exist without some form of organisation. We are surrounded by Churches differing very widely from each other in the principles of their polity: and we have to elect the Church with which we will become associated. New Churches are being founded, and it is necessary to determine how they shall be governed. The question—What form of Church polity is most favourable to the maintenance of a firm and intelligent faith in Christ among the members of the Church, to the increase of their knowledge of Christian truth and duty: to the energy and joy of their spiritual life: to their mutual affection as brothers and sisters in the household of God: to the development of their Christian morality: to the discipline and effective use of whatever powers they possess for the service of God and of mankind?—this is a question which cannot be evaded or postponed.

Dale seeks to answer that question and claims that 'Congregational principles are permanently rooted in the central truths of the Christian revelation, and that the Congregational polity is at once the highest and the most natural organisation of the life of the Christian Church'.

In days of either political anarchy or despotism, it is the Congregational principle of the gathered church subject to

Christ alone which enables a true Scriptural witness to be maintained.

In Congregationalism there is the true 'apostolic succession'. It is not the succession of the consecrating hands of mitred bishops. It is the succession of gospel truth passed from generation to generation by the testimony of men and women who hold the faith of the apostles. We first read of them as those who 'continued steadfastly in the apostles' doctrine' (Acts 2:42) and who were exhorted by Jude to 'earnestly contend for the faith which was once delivered unto the saints'. This 'apostolic succession' is seen in essence in Paul's words to Timothy: 'And the things that thou hast heard of me among many witnesses, the same commit thou to faithful men, who shall be able to teach others also'(2 Timothy 2:2).

At one end of the ecclesiastical spectrum there are the episcopal systems with their hierarchy and ritual. At the other end there are those who make much of their New Testament simplicity. They are strong on Bible teaching and any believer can share in ministry in their simple buildings.

Between these extremes, all that is good and all that is Biblical in the theory and practice of the Church has had its place in the fife and worship of the Congregational Independents. And their story is not done. By the grace of God, and to his glory, the work continues. Dale concluded his *Manual* with a humbling challenge and we would close with his words:

> Never yet, perhaps, has any society gathered together in his name been so perfectly one with him that all its decisions were confirmed by his authority. Congregationalism is an ideal polity. This is at once its reproach and its glory. The transcendent prerogatives and powers which it claims for the church lie beyond the reach of Christian communities which are not completely penetrated and transfigured by the Spirit of Christ. But as churches approach more and more nearly to the perfection to which Christ has called

them, their authority becomes more and more august, and they enter more and more fully into the possession of the blessedness which is their inheritance in him.

*Appendix* 1

# THE SAVOY DECLARATION OF FAITH AND ORDER 1658

With an extract from the original preface by John Owen, and a foreword by Derek Swann, and with Scripture references from the Saybrook Platform.

# CONTENTS

In drawing up this our confession of faith, we have had before us the articles of religion (the Westminster Confession of Faith), approved and passed by both Houses of Parliament, after advice had with an Assembly of Divines called together by them for that purpose. To which confession, for the substance of it, we fully assent, as do our brethren in New England, and the churches also of Scotland, as each in their general synods have testified.

A few things we have added for obviating some erroneous opinions that have been more broadly and boldly maintained of late than in former times; and made some other additions and alterations here and there, and some clearer explanations, as we found occasion.

We have endeavoured throughout to hold to such truths in this our confession as are more properly termed matters of faith; and what is of church order we dispose in certain propositions by itself.

That there are not Scriptures annexed as in some confessions, we give the same account as did the assembly, which was this; The confession being large, and so framed as to meet with the common errors, if the Scripture should have been alleged with any clearness, and by showing where the strength of the proof lay, it would have required a volume.

What we have laid down about churches and their government, we humbly conceive to be the order which Christ has himself appointed to be observed. We have endeavoured to follow Scripture light; and those also that went before us according to that rule.

Our prayer to God is, that whereto we have already attained, we all may walk by the same rule; and that wherein we are otherwise minded, God would reveal it to us in his due time.

From the original preface by John Owen.

# FOREWORD

THE re-publishing of the Savoy Declaration of Faith and Order of 1658 will seem to some rather like the appearance of a penny-farthing bicycle at Cape Kennedy, or a horse-drawn bus in Piccadilly Circus. Both are obsolete, and irrelevant to the 1980s—and so, some would add, is the Savoy Declaration. 'Give it a place in a museum of theology; but keep it out of the world of atomic-powered, space-conscious, modem man', would be the general consensus of opinion.

Prospective readers may therefore feel entitled to some explanation why they should spend their hard-earned money on a 17th-century museum piece of theology. Why have the publishers seen fit to blow away the dust of centuries, crack back the spine and expose, the yellowing pages of the Savoy Declaration to the light of the 20th century?

Firstly, let it be said (very much to our evangelical shame) that there are no other useful modern confessions worthy of publication. No 20th-century Declaration could hold a candle to Savoy, or indeed is even worthy of comparison. The 1833 Congregational Declaration of Faith is simply a shortened version of the Savoy, and the 1967 Declaration published by the then Congregational Union of England and Wales bears, apart from its title, little or no resemblance to its grandfather, the Savoy.

Penny-farthing bicycles are made obsolete only by the appearance of superior pneumatic-tyred machines, and horse-drawn buses are driven into their stables only when displaced by modern petrol-driven vehicles. But what superior Declaration of Faith has appeared to drive the Savoy from the theological scene? The answer is—none! Modernism, with its distaste for theological clarity, is responsible for relegating the Savoy confession to the museum of theology. In its place it has produced anaemic specimens lacking in linguistic (and therefore theological) precision. The 1967 Declaration of Faith is very wordy, but unlike the Savoy with its clarity and precision, it tends to use words to conceal rather than to reveal meaning. This must be so, because its stated belief is that the Christian faith cannot be defined, but only declared.

*Secondly,* our generation needs a comprehensive statement of faith. For too long we have been satisfied with potted knowledge and shrivelled declarations of faith. It would not be an exaggeration to say that some modem evangelicals would be hard put to it to fill a postcard with a clear statement of their faith. The ABC of the gospel is known; but only that. The DEF to Z of the gospel remains a mystery for the majority. We tend to paddle in pools of faith, but never to swim in the sea. We are happy (are we?) with a minimum of knowledge and therefore live impoverished Christian lives. The Savoy is a blessed antidote to such a situation. Not only does it speak of Assurance and Sanctification but also of such neglected matters as Providence, God's Covenant with man, Adoption, Repentance, the Church and the Sacraments. It covers the whole counsel of God, and no one who studies it can fail to be inspired by the breadth of its Scriptural vision.

*Thirdly,* the Savoy is needed because it is a common confession of faith. It is not a barren theological scheme drawn up in an academic manner, but a living confession of the faith of Christians of every age, including those of this 20th century. It is, as John Owen wrote in the original preface, not to be used as an imposition of faith, upon Christians; but rather 'to be looked upon as a fit means to express their common faith and salvation'. Twentieth century evangelicalism is rather like an orchestra in which every musician plays his own tune—to his own personal satisfaction. From this we can expect discordant chaos. That a common tune exists which we can all play (with a few variations) seems not to have occurred to us. The Savoy is a necessary reminder that there is indeed a common tune, and that with God's enabling we can all play it together.

*Fourthly,* the present departure from the 'faith once delivered to the saints' demands a reprint of the Savoy. In the 17th century John Owen wrote: 'Men have taken freedom to vent their own vain and accursed imaginations, contrary to the great and fixed truths of the gospel, insomuch as, taking the whole round and circle of delusions, … it will be found that every truth, of greater or lesser weight, has by one or other hand, at one time or another, been questioned and called to the bar amongst us.' Denial of the great and fixed truths of the gospel is certainly the malaise of the 20th, as well as the 17th century.

Scripture commands us not to remove the old landmarks (Proverbs 22:28). We do so at our own peril. Savoy may be an old landmark; but it is a true and safe one. An old landmark is always to be preferred to no landmark. An old candle-power lighthouse is more precious to the lost atomic-driven submarine than no lighthouse at all. Until a clearer light appears on the horizon we shall be well advised to steer by the clear and safe light of such confessions as the Savoy

Perhaps its re-publication will act as a spur to Christians to re-discover the whole area of truth revealed by God in his Word. It is not an infallible document, but is a more than useful launching-pad for future clarification of the truth, and the deepening of our own knowledge of it.

DEREK SWANN

Ashford, Middlesex

## Chapter 1

# Of the holy Scripture

1 Although the light of nature, and the works of creation and providence, do so far manifest the goodness, wisdom and power of God, as to leave men inexcusable;[1] yet are they not sufficient to give that knowledge of God and of his will, which is necessary unto salvation:[2] therefore it pleased the Lord at sundry times, and in divers manners to reveal himself, and to declare that his will unto his Church;[3] and afterwards for the better preserving and propagating of the truth, and for the more sure establishment and comfort of the Church against the corruption of the flesh, and the malice of Satan and of the world, to commit the same wholly unto writing:[4] which maketh the holy Scripture to be most necessary;[5] those former ways of God's revealing his will unto his people, being now ceased.[6]

---

[1] Romans 2:14,15; Romans 1:19,20; Psalm 19:1,2,3; Romans 1:32; Romans 2:1.

[2] 1 Corinthians 1:21; 2:13,14.

[3] Hebrews 1:1,2.

[4] Proverbs 22:19–21; Luke 1:3,4; Romans 15:4; Matthew 4:4,7,10; Isaiah 8:19,20.

[5] 2 Timothy 3:15; 2 Peter 1:19.

[6] Hebrews 1:1,2.

2 Under the name of holy Scripture, or the Word of God written, are now contained all the Books of the Old and New Testament; which are these:

## Of the Old Testament

Genesis, Exodus, Leviticus, Numbers, Deuteronomy, Joshua, Judges, Ruth, 1 Samuel, 2 Samuel, 1 Kings, 2 Kings, 1 Chronicles, 2 Chronicles, Ezra, Nehemiah, Esther, Job, Psalms, Proverbs, Ecclesiastes, The Song of Songs, Isaiah, Jeremiah, Lamentations. Ezekiel, Daniel, Hosea, Joel, Amos, Obadiah, Jonah, Micah, Nahum, Habakkuk, Zephaniah, Haggai, Zechariah, Malachi.

## Of the New Testament

Matthew, Mark, Luke, John, the Acts of the Apostles, Paul's Epistle to the Romans, 1 Corinthians, 2 Corinthians, Galatians, Ephesians, Philippians, Colossians, 1 Thessalonians, 2 Thessalonians, 1 Timothy, 2 Timothy, Titus, Philemon, the Epistle to the Hebrews, the Epistle of James, the first and second Epistles of Peter, the first, second and third Epistles of John, the Epistle of Jude, the Revelation.

All which are given by the inspiration of God to be the rule of faith and life.[1]

3 The Books commonly called Apocrypha, not being of divine inspiration, are no part of the canon of the Scripture; and therefore are of no authority in the Church of God, nor to be any otherwise approved or made use of, than other human writings.[2]

4 The authority of the holy Scripture, for which it ought to be believed and obeyed, dependeth not upon the testimony of

---

[1] Luke 16:29-31; Ephesians 2:20; Revelation 22:18,19; 2 Timothy 3:16.

[2] Luke 24:27,44; Romans 3:2; 2 Peter 1:21.

any man or church; but wholly upon God (who is Truth itself) the Author thereof: and therefore it is to be received, because it is the Word of God.[1]

5 We may he moved and induced by the testimony of the Church, to an high and reverent esteem of the holy Scripture.[2] And the heavenliness of the matter, the efficacy of the doctrine, the majesty of the style, the consent of all the parts, the scope of the whole (which is, to give all glory to God), the full discovery it makes of the only way of man's salvation, the many other incomparable excellencies, and the entire perfection thereof, are arguments whereby it doth abundantly evidence itself to be the Word of God; yet notwithstanding, our full persuasion and assurance of the infallible truth and divine authority thereof, is from the inward work of the Holy Spirit, bearing witness by and with the Word in our hearts.[3]

6 The whole counsel of God concerning all things necessary for his own glory, man's salvation, faith and life, is either expressly set down in Scripture, or by good and necessary consequence may be deduced from Scripture; unto which nothing at any time is to be added, whether by new revelations of the Spirit, or traditions of men.[4] Nevertheless we acknowledge the inward illumination of the Spirit of God to be necessary for the saving understanding of such things as are revealed in the Word:[5] and that there are some circumstances concerning the worship of God and government of the Church, common to human actions and societies, which are to be ordered by the light of nature and Christian prudence, according to the general rules of the Word, which are always to be observed.[6]

---

[1] 2 Peter 1:19,21; 2 Timothy 3:16; 1 John 5:9; 1 Thessalonians 2:13.

[2] 1 Timothy 3:15.

[3] 1 John 2:20,27; John 16:13,14; 1 Corinthians 2:10–12; Isaiah 59:21.

[4] 2 Timothy 3:15–17; Gal 1:8,9; 2 Thessalonians 2:2,15.

[5] John 6:45; 1 Corinthians 2:9–12.

[6] 1 Corinthians 11:13,14; 14:26,40.

7 All things in Scripture are not alike plain in themselves, nor alike clear unto all:[1] yet those things which are necessary to be known, believed and observed for salvation, are so clearly propounded and opened in some place of Scripture or other, that not only the learned, but the unlearned, in a due use of the ordinary means, may attain unto a sufficient understanding of them.[2]

8 The Old Testament in Hebrew (which was the native language of the people of God of old) and the New Testament in Greek (which at the time of writing of it was most generally known to the nations) being immediately inspired by God, and by his singular care and providence kept pure in all ages, are therefore authentical;[3] so as in all controversies of religion the Church is finally to appeal unto them.[4] But because these original tongues are not known to all the people of God, who have right unto and interest in the Scriptures, and are commanded in the fear of God to read and search them;[5] therefore they are to be translated into the vulgar language of every nation unto which they come,[6] that the Word of God dwelling plentifully in all, they may worship him in an acceptable manner,[7] and through patience and comfort of the Scriptures may have hope.[8]

9 The infallible rule of interpretation of Scripture, is the Scripture itself; and therefore when there is a question about the true and full sense of any Scripture (which is not manifold, but one) it must be searched and known by other places, that speak more clearly.[9]

10 The supreme judge by which all controversies of religion are to be determined, and all decrees of councils, opinions of ancient writers, doctrines of men and private spirits, are to be examined, and in whose sentence we are to rest, can be no other,

---

[1] 2 Peter 3:16.
[2] Psalm 119:105,130; Hebrews 2:2–3.
[3] Matthew 5:18.
[4] Isaiah 8:20; Acts 15:15; John 5:39,46.
[5] John 5:39.
[6] 1 Corinthians 14:6, 9, 11, 12, 24, 27, 28.
[7] Colossians 3:16.
[8] Romans 15:4.
[9] 2 Peter 1:20,21; Acts 15:15,16.

but the holy Scripture delivered by the Spirit; into which Scripture so delivered, our faith is finally resolved.[1]

## *Chapter 2*

# Of God and of the holy Trinity

1 There is but one only[2] living and true God;[3] who is infinite in being and perfection,[4] a most pure Spirit,[5] invisible,[6] without body, parts[7] or passions,[8] immutable,[9] immense,[10] eternal,[11] incomprehensible,[12] almighty,[13] most wise,[14] most holy,[15] most free,[16] most absolute,[17] working all things according to the counsel of his own immutable and most righteous will,[18] for his own glory,[19] most loving,[20] gracious, merciful, long-suffering, abundant in goodness and truth, forgiving iniquity, transgression and sin,[21] the rewarder of them that diligently seek him;[22] and withal most just and terrible in his judgments,[23] hating all sin,[24] and who will by no means clear the guilty.[25]

2 God hath all life,[26] glory,[27] goodness,[28] blessedness,[29] in, and of himself; and is alone, in, and unto himself, all-sufficient, not standing in need of any creatures, which he hath made,[30] nor

---

[1] Matthew 22:29,31; Ephesians 2:20; Acts 28:25.
[2] Deuteronomy 6:4; 1 Corinthians 8:4–6.
[3] 1 Thessalonians 1:9; Jeremiah 10:10.
[4] Job 11:7–9; 26:14.
[5] John 4:24.
[6] 1 Timothy 1:17.
[7] Deuteronomy 4:15,16; John 4:24; Luke 24:39.
[8] Acts 14:11,15.
[9] James 1:17; Malachi 3:6.
[10] 1 Kings 8:27; Jeremiah 23:23,24.
[11] Romans 1:20; 1 Timothy 1:17; Psalm 90:2.
[12] Psalm 145:3.
[13] Genesis 17:1; Revelation 4:8.
[14] Romans 16:27.
[15] Isaiah 6:3; Revelation 4:8.
[16] Psalm 115:3.
[17] Exodus 3:14.
[18] Ephesians 1:11.
[19] Romans 11:36; Proverbs 16:4.
[20] 1 John 4:8,16.
[21] Exodus 34:6,7.
[22] Hebrews 11:6.
[23] Nehemiah 9:32,33.
[24] Psalm 5:5,6.
[25] Exodus 34:7; Nahum 1:2,3.
[26] John 5:26.
[27] Acts 7:2.
[28] Psalm 119:68.
[29] 1 Timothy 6:15; Romans 9:5.
[30] Acts 17:24,25.

deriving any glory from them,[1] but only manifesting his own glory in, by, unto, and upon them: he is the alone fountain of all being, of whom, through whom, and to whom are all things;[2] and hath most sovereign dominion over them, to do by them, for them, or upon them, whatsoever himself pleaseth.[3] In his sight all things are open and manifest,[4] his knowledge is infinite, infallible, and independent upon the creature,[5] so as nothing is to him contingent or uncertain.[6] He is most holy in all his counsels, in all his works, and in all his commands.[7] To him is due from angels and men, and every other creature, whatsoever worship, service or obedience, as creatures, they owe unto the Creator, and whatever he is further pleased to require of them.[8]

3 In the unity of the God-head there be three Persons, of one substance, power and eternity. God the Father, God the Son, and God the Holy Ghost.[9] The Father is of none, neither begotten, nor proceeding; the Son is eternally begotten of the Father;[10] the Holy Ghost eternally proceeding from the Father and the Son.[11] Which doctrine of the Trinity is the foundation of all our communion with God, and comfortable dependence upon him.

## *Chapter* 3

# Of God's Eternal Decree

1 God from all eternity did by the most wise and holy counsel of his own will, freely and unchangeably ordain whatsoever comes to pass:[12] yet so, as thereby neither is God the author of

---

1 Job 22:2,3.
2 Romans 11:36.
3 Revelation 4:11; 1 Timothy 6:15; Daniel 4:25,31,34,35.
4 Hebrews 4:13.
5 Romans 11:33,34; Psalm 147:5.
6 Acts 15:18; Ezekiel 11:5.
7 Psalm 145:17; Romans 7;12.

8 Revelation 5:12–14.
9 1 John 5:7; Matthew 3:16,17; 28:19; 2 Corinthians 13:14.
10 John 1:14,18.
11 John 15:26; Galatians 4:6; 2 Corinthians 13:14.
12 Ephesians 1:11; Romans 11:33; Hebrews 6:17; Romans 9:15,18.

sin,[1] nor is violence offered to the will of the creatures, nor is the liberty or contingency of second causes taken away, but rather established.[2]

2 Although God knows whatsoever may or can come to pass upon all supposed conditions,[3] yet hath he not decreed any thing, because he foresaw it as future, or as that which would come to pass upon such conditions.[4]

3 By the decree of God for the manifestation of his glory, some men and angels[5] are predestinated unto everlasting life, and others fore-ordained to everlasting death.[6]

4 These angels and men thus predestinated, and fore-ordained, are particularly and unchangeably designed, and their number is so certain and definite, that it cannot be either increased or diminished.[7]

5 Those of mankind that are predestinated unto life, God, before the foundation of the world was laid, according to his eternal and immutable purpose, and the secret counsel and good pleasure of his will, hath chosen in Christ unto everlasting glory,[8] out of his mere free grace and love, without any foresight of faith or good works, or perseverance in either of them, or any other thing in the creature, as conditions or causes moving him thereunto,[9] and all to the praise of his glorious grace.[10]

6 As God hath appointed the elect unto glory, so hath he by the eternal and most free purpose of his will fore-ordained all the means thereunto.[11] Wherefore they who are elected, being fallen in Adam, are redeemed by Christ,[12] are effectually called

---

1 James 1:13,17; 1 John 1:5.
2 Acts 2:23; 4:27,28; Matthew 17:12; John 19:11; Proverbs 16:33.
3 Acts 15:18; 23:11,12; Matthew 11:21,23; 1 Samuel 23:11–12
4 Romans 9:11,13,16,18.
5 1 Timothy 5: 21; Matthew 25:41.
6 Romans 9:22,23; Ephesians 1:5–6; Proverbs 16:4.

7 2 Timothy 2:19; John 13:18; John 10:28; Romans 8:28–39
8 Ephesians 1:4,9,11; Romans 8:30; 2 Timothy 1:9; 1 Thessalonians 5:9.
9 Romans 9:11,33; Eph 1:4,9.
10 Ephesians 1:6,12.
11 1 Peter 1:2; Ephesians 1:4,5; 2:10; 2 Thessalonians 2:13.
12 1 Thessalonians 5:9,10; Titus 2:14.

unto faith in Christ by his Spirit working in due season, are justified, adopted, sanctified,[1] and kept by his power, through faith, unto salvation.[2] Neither are any other redeemed by Christ, or effectually called, justified, adopted, sanctified and saved, but the elect only.[3]

7 The rest of mankind God was pleased, according to the unsearchable counsel of his own will, whereby he extendeth or withholdeth mercy, as he pleaseth, for the glory of his sovereign power over his creatures, to pass by and to ordain them to dishonour and wrath for their sin, to the praise of his glorious justice.[4]

8 The doctrine of this high mystery of predestination is to be handled with special prudence and care,[5] that men attending the will of God revealed in his Word, and yielding obedience thereunto, may from the certainty of their effectual vocation, be assured of their eternal election.[6] So shall this doctrine afford matter of praise, reverence and admiration of God,[7] and of humility, diligence, and abundant consolation to all that sincerely obey the Gospel.[8]

## Chapter 4

# Of Creation

1 It pleased God the Father, Son and Holy Ghost,[9] for the manifestation of the glory of his eternal power, wisdom and

---

1 Romans 8:30; Ephesians 1:5; 2 Thessalonians 2:13.

2 1 Peter 1:5.

3 John 17:9; 6:64,65; 8:47; 10:26; Romans 8:28–39; 1 John 2:19.

4 Matthew 11:25,26; Romans 9:17,18,21,22; 2 Timothy 2:19,20; Jude 4; 1 Peter 2:8.

5 Romans 9:20; 11:33; Deuteronomy 29:29.

6 2 Peter 1:10.

7 Ephesians 1:6; Romans 11:33.

8 Romans 11:5,6,20; 2 Peter 1:10; Romans 8:33; Luke 10:20.

9 Hebrews 1:2; John 1:2,3; Genesis 1:2; Job 26:13; 33:4.

goodness,[1] in the beginning, to create or make out of nothing the world, and all things therein, whether visible or invisible, in the space of six days, and all very good.[2]

2 After God had made all other creatures, he created man, male and female,[3] with reasonable and immortal souls,[4] endued with knowledge, righteousness and true holiness, after his own image,[5] having the law of God written in their hearts,[6] and power to fulfil it;[7] and yet under a possibility of transgressing, being left to the liberty of their own will, which was subject unto change.[8] Besides this law written in their hearts, they received a command not to eat of the tree of the knowledge of good and evil; which while they kept, they were happy in their communion with God,[9] and had dominion over the creatures.[10]

## *Chapter* 5

# Of Providence

1 God the great Creator of all things, doth uphold,[11] direct, dispose and govern all creatures, actions and things[12] from the greatest even to the least[13] by his most wise and holy providence,[14] according unto his infallible foreknowledge,[15] and the free and immutable counsel of his own will,[16] to the praise of the glory of his wisdom, power, justice, goodness and mercy.[17]

---

1 Romans 1:20; Jeremiah 10:12; Psalm 104:24; 33:5,6.
2 Genesis 1:1–31; Hebrews 11:3; Colossians 1:16; Acts 17:24.
3 Genesis 1:27.
4 Genesis 2:7; Ecclesiastes 12:7; Luke 23:43; Matthew 10:28.
5 Genesis 1:26; Colossians 3:10; Ephesians 4:24.
6 Romans 2:14,15.
7 Ecclesiastes 7:29.
8 Genesis 3:6; Ecclesiastes 7:29.
9 Genesis 3:8–11,23; 2:17
10 Genesis 1:26,28; 2:17.
11 Hebrews 1:3.
12 Daniel 4:34,35; Psalm 135:6; Acts 17:25,26,28,29; Job 38:1–41:3.
14 Matthew 10:29–31.
15 Psalm 104:24; 145:17; Proverbs 15:3
16 Acts 15:18; Psalm 94:8–11.
17 Ephesians 1:11; Psalm 33:10,11.
18 Isaiah 63:14; Ephesians 3:10; Romans 9:17; Genesis 45:7; Psalm 145:17.

2 Although in relation to the foreknowledge and decree of God, the first cause, all things come to pass immutably and infallibly;[1] yet by the same providence he ordereth them to fall out according to the nature of second causes, either necessarily, freely, or contingently.[2]

3 God in his ordinary providence maketh use of means,[3] yet is free to work without,[4] above,[5] and against them at his pleasure.[6]

4 The almighty power, unsearchable wisdom, and infinite goodness of God, so far manifest themselves in his providence, in that his determinate counsel extendeth itself even to the first fall, and all other sins of angels and men[7] (and that not by a bare permission[8]) which also he most wisely and powerfully boundeth,[9] and otherwise ordereth and governeth in a manifold dispensation to his own most holy ends;[10] yet so, as the sinfulness thereof proceedeth only from the creature, and not from God, who being most holy and righteous, neither is, nor can be the author or approver of sin.[11]

5 The most wise, righteous and gracious God doth oftentimes leave for a season his own children to manifold temptations, and the corruption of their own hearts, to chastise them for their former sins, or to discover unto them the hidden strength of corruption, and deceitfulness of their hearts, that they may be humbled;[12] and to raise them to a more close and constant dependence for their support upon himself, and to make them

---

1 Acts 2:23.

2 Jeremiah 31:35; Exodus 21:13; Genesis 8:22; Deuteronomy 19:5; 1 Kings 22:28,34.

3 Acts 27:31,44; Isaiah 55:10–11; Hosea 2:21,22.

4 Hosea 1:7; Matthew 4:4; Job 34:10.

5 Romans 4:19–21.

6 2 Kings 6:6; Daniel 3:27.

7 Romans 11:32–34; 2 Samuel 24:1 with 1 Chronicles 21:1; 1 Kings 22:22,23; 1 Chronicles 10:4,13,14; 2 Samuel 16:10; Acts 2:23; 4:27,28.

8 Acts 14:16.

9 Psalm 76:10; 2 Kings 19:28.

10 Genesis 50:20; Isaiah 10:6,7,12.

11 James 1:13,14,17; 1 John 2:16; Psalm 50:21.

12 2 Chronicles 32:25,26,31; 2 Samuel 24:1.

more watchful against all future occasions of sin, and for sundry other just and holy ends.[1]

6 As for those wicked and ungodly men, whom God as a righteous judge, for former sins, doth blind and harden,[2] from them he not only withholdeth his grace, whereby they might have been enlightened in their understandings, and wrought upon in their hearts;[3] but sometimes also withdraweth the gifts which they had,[4] and exposeth them to such objects, as their corruption makes occasions of sin;[5] and withal gives them over to their own lusts, the temptations of the world, and the power of Satan;[6] whereby it comes to pass that they harden themselves, even under those means which God useth for the softening of others.[7]

7 As the providence of God doth in general reach to all creatures, so after a most special manner it taketh care of his Church, and disposeth all things to the good thereof.[8]

## Chapter 6

# Of the fall of Man, of Sin, and of the Punishment thereof

1 God having made a covenant of works and life, thereupon,[9] with our first parents and all their posterity in them,[10] they being seduced by the subtlety and temptation of Satan did

---

1 2 Corinthians 12:7–9; Psalm 73:1–28; Psalm 77:1–12; Mark 14:66-72; John 21:15,16,17.
2 Romans 1:24,26,28; Romans 11:7,8.
3 Deuteronomy 29:4
4 Matthew 13:12; Matthew 25:29.
5 Deuteronomy 2:30; 2 Kings 8:12,13.
6 Psalm 81:11–12; 2 Thessalonians 2:10–12.
7 Exodus 7:3; 8:15,32; 2 Corinthians 2:14–16; Isaiah 8:14; 1 Peter 2:7,8; Isaiah 6:9,10; Acts 28:26.
8 1 Timothy 4:10; Amos 9:8,9; Romans 8:28; Isaiah 43:3–5,14.
9 Romans 10:5.
10 Romans 5:12,13; 1 Corinthians 15:21,22; Leviticus 18:5.

wilfully transgress the law of their creation, and break the covenant in eating the forbidden fruit.[1]

2 By this sin they, and we in them, fell from original righteousness and communion with God,[2] and so became dead in sin,[3] and wholly defiled in all the faculties and parts of soul and body.[4]

3 They being the root, and by God's appointment standing in the room and stead of all mankind, the guilt of this sin was imputed,[5] and corrupted nature conveyed to all their posterity descending from them by ordinary generation.[6]

4 From this original corruption, whereby we are utterly indisposed, disabled and made opposite to all good,[7] and wholly inclined to all evil,[8] do proceed all actual transgressions.[9]

5 This corruption of nature during this life, doth remain in those that are regenerated;[10] and although it be through Christ pardoned and mortified, yet both itself and all the motions thereof are truly and properly sin.[11]

6 Every sin, both original and actual, being a transgression of the righteous law of God, and contrary thereunto,[12] doth in its own nature bring guilt upon the sinner,[13] whereby he is bound over to the wrath of God,[14] and curse of the law,[15] and so made subject to death,[16] with all miseries, spiritual,[17] temporal[18] and eternal.[19]

---

1 Genesis 3:13; 2 Corinthians 11:3.
2 Genesis 3:6–8; Ecclesiastes 7:29; Romans 3:23.
3 Genesis 2:17; Ephesians 2:1.
4 Titus 1:15; Genesis 6:5; Jeremiah 17:9; Romans 3:10–19.
5 Genesis 1:27,28; 2:16,17; Acts 17:26; Romans 5:12,15–19; 1 Corinthians 15:21,22,45,49.
6 Psalm 51:5; Genesis 5:3; Job 14:4; 15:14.
7 Romans 5:6; 8:7; 7:18; Colossians 1:21.
8 Genesis 6:5; 8:21; Romans 3:10–12.
9 James 1:14,15; Ephesians 2:2,3; Matthew 15:19.

10 1 John 1:8,10; Romans 7:14,17,18,23; James 3:2; Proverbs 20:9; Ecclesiastes 7:20.
11 Romans 7:5,7,8,24,25; Galatians 5:17.
12 1 John 3:4.
13 Romans 2:15; 3:9,19.
14 Ephesians 2:3.
15 Galatians 3:10.
16 Romans 6:23.
17 Ephesians 4:18.
18 Romans 8:20; Lam. 3:39.
19 Matthew 25:41; 2 Thessalonians 1:9.

## *Chapter 7*

# Of God's Covenant with Man

1 The distance between God and the creature is so great, that although reasonable creatures do owe obedience unto him as their Creator, yet they could never have attained the reward of life, but by some voluntary condescension on God's part, which he hath been pleased to express by way of covenant.[1]

2 The first covenant made with man, was a covenant of works,[2] wherein life was promised to Adam, and in him to his posterity,[3] upon condition of perfect and personal obedience.[4]

3 Man by his fall having made himself incapable of life by that covenant, the Lord was pleased to make a second,[5] commonly called the Covenant of Grace; wherein he freely offereth unto sinners life and salvation by Jesus Christ, requiring of them faith in him that they may be saved,[6] and promising to give unto all those that are ordained unto life, his Holy Spirit, to make them willing and able to believe.[7]

4 This covenant of grace is frequently set forth in the Scripture by the name of a Testament, in reference to the death of Jesus Christ the testator, and to the everlasting inheritance, with all things belonging to it, therein bequeathed.[8]

5 Although this covenant hath been differently and variously administered in respect of ordinances and institutions in the time of the law, and since the coming of Christ in the flesh;[9]

---

1 Isaiah 40:13–17; Job 9:32,33; Psalm 113:5,6; 100:2,3; Job 22:2,3; 35:7,8; Luke 17:10; Acts 17:24,25; 1 Samuel 2:25.

2 Galatians 3:12.

3 Romans 10:5; 5:12–20.

4 Genesis 2:17; Galatians 3:10.

5 Galatians 3:21; Romans 3:20,21; Genesis 3:5; Isaiah 42:6; Romans 8:3.

6 Mark 16:15,16; John 3:16; Romans 10:6,9,10; Galatians 3:11.

7 Ezekiel 36:26,27; John 6:44,45.

8 Hebrews 7:22; 9:15–17; Luke 22:20; 1 Corinthians 11:25.

9 2 Corinthians 3:6–9; Hebrews 8:1–10:39; 12:18–24; Colossians 2:11,12; 1 Corinthians 5:7,8; 10:25.

yet for the substance and efficacy of it, to all its spiritual and saving ends, it is one and the same;[1] upon the account of which various dispensations, it is called the Old and New Testament.[2]

## Chapter 8

# Of Christ the Mediator

1 It pleased God, in his eternal purpose, to choose and ordain the Lord Jesus his only begotten Son, according to a covenant made between them both, to be the Mediator between God and man;[3] the Prophet,[4] Priest,[5] and King,[6] the Head and Saviour of his Church,[7] the Heir of all things[8] and Judge of the world;[9] unto whom he did from all eternity give a people to be his seed,[10] and to be by him in time redeemed, called, justified, sanctified, and glorified.[11]

2 The Son of God, the second Person in the Trinity, being very and eternal God, of one substance and equal with the Father, did, when the fullness of time was come, take upon him man's nature,[12] with all the essential properties and common infirmities thereof, yet without sin,[13] being conceived by the power of the Holy Ghost, in the womb of the virgin Mary, of her substance:[14] So that two whole perfect and distinct natures, the Godhead and the manhood, were inseparably joined together in one Person, without conversion, composition, or confusion;[15] which

---

1 Galatians 3:3; Ephesians 4:5; Romans 3:21,22,30; 1:16.
2 2 Corinthians 3:6,14.
3 Isaiah 42:1; 1 Peter 1:19,20; John 3:16; 1 Timothy 2:5.
4 Acts 3:22.
5 Hebrews 5:5,6.
6 Psalm 2:6; Luke 1:33.
7 Ephesians 5:23.
8 Hebrews 1:2.
9 Acts 17:31.

10 John 17:6; Psalm 22:30; Isaiah 53:10.
11 1 Timothy 2:6; Isaiah 55:4–5; 1 Corinthians 1:30.
12 John 1:1,14,17; Philippians 2:6; Galatians 4:4; 1 John 5:20
13 Hebrews 2:14,16,17; 4:15.
14 Luke 1:27,31,35; Gal 4:4.
15 Luke 1:35; Romans 9:5; Colossians 2:9; 1 Peter 3:18; 1 Timothy 3:16.

Person is very God and very man, yet one Christ, the only Mediator between God and man.[1]

3 The Lord Jesus in his human nature, thus united to the divine in the Person of the Son, was sanctified and anointed with the Holy Spirit above measure,[2] having in him all the treasures of wisdom and knowledge,[3] in whom it pleased the Father that all fullness should dwell;[4] to the end that being holy, harmless, undefiled, and full of grace and truth,[5] he might be throughly furnished to execute the office of a Mediator and Surety;[6] which office he took not unto himself, but was thereunto called by his Father,[7] who also put all power and judgment into his hand, and gave him commandment to execute the same.[8]

4 This office the Lord Jesus did most willingly undertake;[9] which that he might discharge, he was made under the law,[10] and did perfectly fulfil it,[11] and underwent the punishment due to us, which we should have borne and suffered, being made sin and a curse for us, enduring most grievous torments immediately from God in his soul,[12] and most painful sufferings in his body,[13] was crucified, and died;[14] was buried, and remained under the power of death, yet saw no corruption.[14] On the third day he arose from the dead[16] with the same body in which he suffered,[17] with which also he ascended into heaven, and there sitteth at the right hand of his Father,[18] making intercession;[19] and shall return to judge men and angels at the end of the world.[20]

---

1 Romans 1:3; 1 Timothy 2:5.
2 Psalm 45:7; John 3:34.
3 Colossians 2:3.
4 Colossians 1:19.
5 Hebrews 7:26; John 1:14.
6 Acts 10:38; Hebrews 12:24; 7:22.
7 Hebrews 5:4,5.
8 John 5:21,22,27; Matthew 28:18; Acts 2:36.
9 Psalm 40:7,8; Hebrews 10:5–10; John 10:18; Philippians 2:8.
10 Galatians 4:4.
11 Matthew 3:15; 5:17.
12 Matthew 26:37,38; 27:46; Luke 22:44.
13 Matthew 26:1–27,66.
14 Philippians 2:8.
15 Acts 2:23,24,27; 13:37; Romans 6:9.
16 1 Corinthians 15:3,4.
17 John 20:25,27.
18 Mark 16:19.
19 Rom 8:34; Hebrews 9:24; 7:25.
20 Romans 14:9,10; Acts 1:11; 10:42; Matthew 13:40–42; Jude 6; 2 Peter 2:4.

5 The Lord Jesus by his perfect obedience and sacrifice of himself, which he through the eternal Spirit, once offered up unto God, hath fully satisfied the justice of God,[1] and purchased not only reconciliation, but an everlasting inheritance in the kingdom of heaven, for all those whom the Father hath given unto him.[2]

6 Although the work of redemption was not actually wrought by Christ, till after his incarnation; yet the virtue, efficacy and benefits thereof were communicated to the elect in all ages, successively from the beginning of the world, in and by those promises, types and sacrifices wherein he was revealed and signified to be the Seed of the woman, which should bruise the serpent's head, and the Lamb slain from the beginning of the world, being yesterday and today the same, and for ever.[3]

7 Christ in the work of mediation acteth according to both natures; by each nature doing that which is proper to itself;[4] yet by reason of the unity of the Person, that which is proper to one nature, is sometimes in Scripture attributed to the Person denominated by the other nature.[5]

8 To all those for whom Christ hath purchased redemption, he doth certainly and effectually apply and communicate the same;[6] making intercession for them;[7] and revealing unto them in and by the Word, the mysteries of salvation;[8] effectually persuading them by his Spirit to believe and obey, and governing their hearts by his Word and Spirit;[9] overcoming all their enemies by his almighty power and wisdom, and in such manner and

---

1 Romans 5:19; Hebrews 9:14,16; 10:14; Ephesians 5:2; Romans 3:25,26.

2 Colossians 1:19,20; Daniel 9:24,26; Ephesians 1:11,14; John 17:2; Hebrews 9:12,15.

3 Galatians 4:4,5; Genesis 3:15; Revelation 13:8; Hebrews 13:8.

4 Hebrews 9:14,15; 1 Peter 3:18.

5 Acts 20:28; John 3:13; 1 John 3:16.

6 John 6:37,39; 10:15,16.

7 1 John 2:1; Romans 8:34.

8 John 15:13,15; Ephesians 1:7–9; John 17:6.

9 John 14:16; Hebrews 12:2; 2 Corinthians 4:13; Romans 8:9,14; 15:18,19; John 17:17.

ways as are most consonant to his most wonderful and unsearchable dispensation.[1]

## *Chapter 9*

# Of Free-will

1 God hath endued the will of man with that natural liberty and power of acting upon choice that it is neither forced, nor by any absolute necessity of nature determined to do good or evil.[2]

2 Man in his state of innocency had freedom and power to will and to do that which was good and well-pleasing to God;[3] but yet mutably, so that he might fall from it.[4]

3 Man by his fall into a state of sin, hath wholly lost all ability of will to any spiritual good accompanying salvation;[5] so as a natural man being altogether averse from that good,[6] and dead in sin,[7] is not able by his own strength to convert himself, or to prepare himself thereunto.[8]

4 When God converts a sinner, and translates him into the state of grace, he freeth him from his natural bondage under sin,[9] and by his grace alone enables him freely to will and to do that which is spiritually good;[10] yet so as that, by reason of his remaining corruption, he doth not perfectly nor only will that which is good, but doth also will that which is evil.[11]

5 The will of man is made perfectly and immutably free to do good alone in the state of glory only.[12]

---

1 Psalm 110:1; 1 Corinthians 15:25,26; Malachi 4:2,3; Colossians 2:15.
2 Matthew 17:12; James 1:14; Deuteronomy 30:19.
3 Genesis 1:26; Ecclesiastes 7:29.
4 Genesis 2:16,17; 3:6
5 Romans 5:6; 8:7; John 15:5.
6 Romans 3:10,12.
7 Ephesians 2:1,5; Colossians 2:13.

8 John 6:44,65; Ephesians 2:2–5; 1 Corinthians 2:14; Titus 3:3–5.
9 Colossians 1:13; Philippians 2:13; John 8:34.
10 Romans 6:18,22; Philippians 2:13.
11 Galatians 5:17; Romans 7:15,18,19,21, 23.
12 1 John 3:2; Jude 24; Ephesians 4:13; Hebrews 12:23.

## *Chapter* 10

# Of Effectual Calling

1 All those whom God hath predestinated unto life, and those only, he is pleased in his appointed and accepted time effectually to call[1] by his Word and Spirit,[2] out of that state of sin and death in which they are by nature, to grace and salvation by Jesus Christ;[3] enlightening their minds spiritually and savingly to understand the things of God,[4] taking away their heart of stone, and giving unto them an heart of flesh;[5] renewing their wills, and by his almighty power determining them to that which is good;[6] and effectually drawing them to Jesus Christ;[7] yet so, as they come most freely, being made willing by his grace.[8]

2 This effectual call is of God's free and special grace alone, not from any thing at all foreseen in man,[9] who is altogether passive therein, until being quickened and renewed by the Holy Spirit[10] he is thereby enabled to answer this call, and to embrace the grace offered and conveyed in it.[11]

3 Elect infants dying in infancy, are regenerated and saved by Christ,[12] who worketh when, and where, and how he pleaseth:[13] so also are all other elect persons who are incapable of being outwardly called by the ministry of the Word.[14]

---

1 Romans 8:30; 11:7; Ephesians 1:10,11.
2 2 Thessalonians 2:13,14; 2 Corinthians 3:3,6.
3 Romans 8:2,7; Ephesians 2:1–5; 2 Timothy 1:9,10.
4 Acts 26:18; Colossians 2:10,11; Ephesians 1:17,18; 1 Corinthians 2:10–12.
5 Ezekiel 36:26.
6 Ezekiel 11:19; Philippians 2:13; Deuteronomy 30:6; Ezekiel 36:27.
7 Ephesians 1:19; John 6:44,45.

8 Song of Solomon 1:4; Psalm 110:3; John 6:37; Romans 6:16,17,18.
9 2 Timothy 1:9; Titus 3:4,5; Ephesians 2:4,5,8,9; Romans 9:11.
10 1 Corinthians 2:14; Romans 8:7; Ephesians 2:5.
11 John 6:37; Ezekiel 36:27; Romans 8:9; John 5:25.
12 Luke 18:15,16; Acts 2:38,39; John 3:3,5; 1 John 5:12; Romans 8:9.
13 John 3:8.
14 1 John 5:12; Acts 4:12.

4 Others not elected, although they may be called by the ministry of the Word,[1] and may have some common operations of the Spirit,[2] yet not being effectually drawn by the Father, they neither do nor can come unto Christ, and therefore cannot be saved:[3] much less can men not professing the Christian religion, be saved in any other way whatsoever, be they never so diligent to frame their lives according to the light of nature, and the law of that religion they do profess:[4] and to assert and maintain that they may, is very pernicious, and to be detested.[5]

## Chapter 11

# Of Justification

1 Those whom God effectually calleth, he also freely justifieth;[6] not by infusing righteousness into them, but by pardoning their sins, and by accounting and accepting their persons as righteous; not for anything wrought in them, or done by them, but for Christ's sake alone; nor by imputing faith itself, the act of believing, or any other evangelical obedience to them, as their righteousness; but by imputing Christ's active obedience unto the whole law, and passive obedience in his death for their whole and sole righteousness,[7] they receiving and resting on him and his righteousness by faith; which faith they have not of themselves, it is the gift of God.[8]

2 Faith thus receiving and resting on Christ, and his righteousness, is the alone instrument of justification;[9] yet it is not alone in

---

1 Matthew 22:14.

2 Matthew 7:22; 13:20,21; Hebrews 6:4,5.

3 John 6:64–66; 8:24.

4 Acts 4:12; John 14:6; Ephesians 2:12; John 4:22; 17:3.

5 2 John 9–11; 1 Corinthians 16:22; Galatians 1:6–8.

6 Romans 8:30; 3:24.

7 Jeremiah 23:6; 1 Corinthians 1:30,31; Romans 5:17–19.

8 Acts 10:43–44; Galatians 2:16; Philippians 3:9; Acts 13:38,39; Ephesians 2:7,8.

9 John 1:12; Romans 3:28; 5:1.

the person justified, but is ever accompanied with all other saving graces, and is no dead faith, but worketh by love.[1]

3 Christ by his obedience and death did fully discharge the debt of all those that are justified, and did by the sacrifice of himself, in the blood of his cross, undergoing in their stead the penalty due unto them make a proper, real, and full satisfaction to God's justice in their behalf.[2] Yet in as much as he was given by the Father for them,[3] and his obedience and satisfaction accepted in their stead,[4] and both freely, not for any thing in them, their justification is only of free grace,[5] that both the exact justice and rich grace of God might be glorified in the justification of sinners.[6]

4 God did from all eternity decree to justify all the elect,[7] and Christ did in the fulness of time die for their sins, and rise again for their justification:[8] nevertheless, they are not justified personally, until the Holy Spirit doth in due time actually apply Christ unto them.[9]

5 God doth continue to forgive the sins of those that are justified;[10] and although they can never fall from the state of justification,[11] yet they may by their sins fall under God's fatherly displeasure: and in that condition they have not usually the light of his countenance restored unto them, until they humble themselves, confess their sins, beg pardon, and renew their faith and repentance.[12]

---

1 James 2:17,22,26; Galatians 5:6.
2 Romans 5:8–10,19; 1 Timothy 2:5,6; Hebrews 10:10,14; Daniel 9:24,26; Isaiah 53:4–6,10–12.
3 Romans 8:32.
4 2 Corinthians 5:21; Matthew 3:17; Ephesians 5:2.
5 Romans 3:24; Ephesians 1:7.
6 Romans 3:26; Ephesians 2:7.

7 Galatians 3:8; 1 Peter 1:2,19,20; Romans 8:30.
8 Galatians 4:4; 1 Timothy 2:6; Romans 4:25.
9 Colossians 1:21,22; Galatians 2:16; Titus 3:3–7.
10 Matthew 6:12; 1 John 1:7,9; 2:1,2.
11 Luke 12:32; John 10:28; Hebrews 10:14.
12 Psalm 89:31–33; 51:7–12; 32:5; Matthew 26:75; 1 Corinthians 11:30–32; Luke 1:20.

6 The justification of believers under the Old Testament, was in all these respects one and the same with the justification of believers under the New Testament.[1]

## *Chapter* 12

# Of Adoption

1 All those that are justified, God vouchsafeth in and for his only Son Jesus Christ to make partakers of the grace of adoption,[2] by which they are taken into the number, and enjoy the liberties and privileges of the children of God,[3] have his name put upon them,[4] receive the Spirit of adoption;[5] have access to the throne of grace with boldness,[6] are enabled to cry, Abba Father;[7] are pitied,[8] protected,[9] provided for,[10] and chastened by him as by a.father;[11] yet never cast off,[12] but sealed to the day of redemption,[13] and inherit the promises[14] as heirs of everlasting salvation.[15]

## *Chapter* 13

# Of Sanctification

1 They that are united to Christ, effectually called and regenerated, having a new heart and a new spirit created in them, through the virtue of Christ's death and resurrection,[16]

---

1 Galatians 3:8,9,13,14; Romans 4:22–24; Hebrews 13:8.
2 Ephesians 1:5.
3 Galatians 4: 4,5; Romans 8:17; John 1:12.
4 Jeremiah 14:9; 2 Corinthians 6:18; Revelation 3:12.
5 Romans 8:15.
6 Ephesians 3:12; Romans. 5:2.
7 Galatians 4:6.

8 Psalm 103:13.
9 Proverbs 14:26.
10 Matthew 6:30,32; 1 Peter 5:7.
11 Hebrews 12:6.
12 Lamentations 3:31.
13 Ephesians 4:30.
14 Hebrews 6:12.
15 1 Peter 1:3,4; Hebrews 1:14.
16 1 Corinthians 6:11; Acts 20:32; Philippians 3:10; Romans 6:5,6.

are also further sanctified really and personally through the same virtue, by his Word and Spirit dwelling in them;[1] the dominion of the whole body of sin is destroyed[2] and the several lusts thereof are more and more weakened, and mortified,[3] and they more and more quickened, and strengthened in all saving graces,[4] to the practice of all true holiness, without which no man shall see the Lord.[5]

2 This sanctification is throughout in the whole man,[6] yet imperfect in this life; there abideth still some remnants of corruption in every part;[7] whence ariseth a continual and irreconcilable war, the flesh lusting against the Spirit, and the Spirit against the flesh.[8]

3 In which war, although the remaining corruption for a time may much prevail,[9] yet through the continual supply of strength from the sanctifying Spirit of Christ, the regenerate part doth overcome,[10] and so the saints grow in grace,[11] perfecting holiness in the fear of God.[12]

## Chapter 14

# Of saving Faith

1 The grace of faith, whereby the elect are enabled to believe to the saving of their souls,[13] is the work of the Spirit of Christ in their hearts,[14] and is ordinarily wrought by the ministry of

---

1 John 17:17; Ephesians 5:26; 2 Thessalonians 2:13.
2 Romans 6:6,14.
3 Galatians 5:24; Romans 8:13.
4 Colossians 1:11; Ephesians 3:16–19.
5 2 Corinthians 7:1; Hebrews 12:14.
6 1 Thessalonians 5:23.
7 1 John 1:10; Romans 7:18,23; Philippians 3:12.

8 Galatians 5:17; 1 Peter 2:11.
9 Romans 7:23.
10 Romans 6:14; 1 John 5:4; Ephesians 4:15,16.
11 2 Peter 3:18; 2 Corinthians 3:18.
12 2 Corinthians 3:18; 7:1.
13 Hebrews 10:39.
14 2 Corinthians 4:13; Ephesians 1:17–19; 2:8.

the Word;[1] by which also, and by the administration of the seals, prayer, and other means, it is increased and strengthened.[2]

2 By this faith a Christian believeth to be true whatsoever is revealed in the Word, for the authority of God himself speaking therein,[3] and acteth differently upon that which each particular passage thereof containeth; yielding obedience to the commands,[4] trembling at the threatenings, and embracing the promises of God for this life, and that which is to come.[5] But the principal acts of saving faith are, accepting, receiving, and resting upon Christ alone, for justification, sanctification, and eternal life, by virtue of the covenant of grace.[6]

3 This faith, although it be different in degrees, and may be weak or strong[7] yet it is in the least degree of it different in the kind or nature of it (as is all other saving grace) from the faith and common grace of temporary believers;[8] and therefore, though it may be many times assailed and weakened, yet it gets the victory,[9] growing up in many to the attainment of a full assurance through Christ,[10] who is both the author and finisher of our faith.[11]

## *Chapter* 15

# Of Repentance unto life and salvation

1 Such of the elect as are converted at riper years, having sometime lived in the state of nature, and therein served divers

---

1  Romans 10:14,17; Acts 20:32; Romans 4:11; Luke 17:5; Romans 1:16,17.
2  1 Peter 2:2.
3  John 4:42; 1 Thessalonians 2:13; 1 John 5:10; Acts 24:14.
4  Romans 16:26.
5  Hebrews 11:13; 1 Timothy 4:8.
6  John 1:12; Acts 16:31; Galatians 2:20; Acts 15:11.

7  Hebrews 5:13,14; Romans 4:19,20; Matthew 6:30; 8:10.
8  Job 8:13; 1 John 3:9.
9  Luke 22:31,32; Ephesians 6:16; 1 John 5:4,5.
10 Hebrews 6:11,12; 10:22; Colossians 2:2.
11 Hebrews 12:2.

lusts and pleasures,[1] God in their effectual calling giveth them repentance unto life.[2]

2 Whereas there is none that doth good, and sinneth not,[3] and the best of men may through the power and deceitfulness of their corruptions dwelling in them,[4] with the prevalency of temptation,[5] fall into great sins and provocations;[6] God hath in the covenant of grace mercifully provided, that believers so sinning and falling, be renewed through repentance unto salvation.[7]

3 This saving repentance is an evangelical grace,[8] whereby a person being by the Holy Ghost made sensible of the manifold evils of his sin,[9] doth by faith in Christ humble himself for it with godly sorrow, detestation of it, and self-abhorrence,[10] praying for pardon and strength of grace,[11] with a purpose, and endeavour by supplies of the Spirit, to walk before God unto all well-pleasing in all things.[12]

4 As repentance is to be continued through the whole course of our lives,[13] upon the account of the body of death, and the motions thereof;[14] so it is every man's duty to repent of his particular known sins particularly.[15]

5 Such is the provision which God hath made through Christ in the covenant of grace, for the preservation of believers unto salvation,[16] that although there is no sin so small, but it deserves damnation;[17] yet there is no sin so great, that it shall bring

---

1 Ephesians 2:1–3; Titus 3:3–5; 1 Peter 4:3.
2 Romans 8:30; 2 Timothy 1:9; Acts 11:18.
3 1 Kings 8:46; Ecclesiastes 7:20; James 3:2.
4 Psalm 65:3; 40:12; Romans 7:21,23; Jeremiah 17:9; Hebrews 3:13.
5 Matthew 6:13; Luke 22:31.
6 2 Samuel 11:27; Luke 22:57,58,60.
7 Luke 22:32,61,62; 1 John 1:9.
8 Zechariah 12:10; Acts 11:18.
9 John 16:7–9; Ezekiel 18:30,31; 36:31; Psalm 51:4; 1 John 3:4.

10 Zechariah 12:10; Jeremiah 31:18,19; Joel 2:12,13; Isaiah 30:22; Amos 5:15; Psalm 119:128; Ezekiel 6:9; 2 Corinthians 7:11.
11 Psalm 51.
12 Psalm 119:6,9,106; 2 Kings 23:25; Colossians 1:10.
13 Matthew 6:11,12; Psalm 51:17.
14 Romans 7:14,15,17–21,23,24; Galatians 5:17.
15 Psalm 19:13; 18:23; 51:4; Luke 19:8; 1 Timothy 1:13,15.
16 1 Peter 1:5.
17 Romans 6:23; 5:12; Matthew 12:36.

damnation on them who truly repent;[1] which makes the constant preaching of repentance necessary.[2]

## Chapter 16

# Of good Works

1 Good works are only such as God hath commanded in his holy Word,[3] and not such as without the warrant thereof are devised by men out of blind zeal, or upon pretence of good intentions.[4]

2 These good works done in obedience to God's commandments, are the fruits and evidences of a true and lively faith;[5] and by them believers manifest their thankfulness,[6] strengthen their assurance,[7] edify their brethren,[8] adorn the profession of the gospel,[9] stop the mouths of the adversaries,[10] and glorify God,[11] whose workmanship they are, created in Christ Jesus thereunto;[12] that having their fruit unto holiness, they may have the end, eternal life.[13]

3 Their ability to do good works is not at all of themselves, but wholly from the Spirit of Christ:[14] And that they may be enabled thereunto, besides the graces they have already received, there is required an actual influence of the same Holy Spirit to work in them to will and to do of his good pleasure;[15] yet are they not hereupon to grow negligent, as if they were not bound

---

1 Isaiah 55:7; Romans 8:1; Isaiah 1:16,18.
2 Mark 1: 15; Acts 20:21.
3 Micah 6:8; Romans 12:2; Hebrews 13:21.
4 Matthew 15:9; Isaiah 29:13; Romans 10:2; Job 16:2; 1 Samuel 15:21–23; 1 Peter 1:18.
5 James 2:18,22.
6 Psalm 116:12,13; 1 Peter 2:9.

7 1 John 2:3,5; 2 Peter 1:5–10; 2:9,10.
8 2 Corinthians 9:2; Matthew 5:16.
9 Titus 2:5,9–12; 1 Timothy 6:1
10 1 Peter 2:15.
11 1 Peter 2:12; Philippians 1:11; John 15:8.
12 Ephesians 2:10.
13 Romans 6:22.
14 John 15:4,6; Ezekiel 36:26,27.
15 Philippians 2:13; 4:13; 2 Corinthians 3:5.

to perform any duty unless upon a special motion of the Spirit; but they ought to be diligent in stirring up the grace of God that is in them.[1]

4 They who in their obedience attain to the greatest height which is possible in this life, are so far from being able to supererogate, and to do more than God requires, as that they fall short of much which in duty they are bound to do.[2]

5 We cannot by our best works merit pardon of sin, or eternal life at the hand of God, by reason of the great disproportion that is between them and the glory to come; and the infinite distance that is between us and God, whom by them we can neither profit, nor satisfy for the debt of our former sins;[3] but when we have done all we can, we have done but our duty, and are unprofitable servants;[4] and because, as they are good, they proceed from the Spirit,[5] and as they are wrought by us, they are defiled and mixed with so much weakness and imperfection, that they cannot endure the severity of God's judgment.[6]

6 Yet notwithstanding, the persons of believers being accepted through Christ, their good works also are accepted in him;[7] not as though they were in this life wholly unblameable and unreproveable in God's sight;[8] but that he looking upon them in his Son is pleased to accept and reward that which is sincere, although accompanied with many weaknesses and imperfections.[9]

7 Works done by unregenerate men, although for the matter of them they may be things which God commands, and of good

---

1 Philippians 2:12; Hebrews 6:11,12; 2 Peter 1:3,5,10,11; Isaiah 64:7; 2 Timothy 1:6.

2 Luke 17:10; Nehemiah 13:22; Job 9:2,3; Galatians 5:17.

3 Romans 3:20; 4:2,4,6; Ephesians 2:8,9; Titus 3:5–7; Romans 8:18; Psalm 16:2; Job 22:2,3.

4 Luke 17:10.

5 Galatians 5:22,23.

6 Isaiah 64:6; Galatians 5:17; Romans 7:15,18; Psalm 143:2; 130:3.

7 Ephesians 1:6; 1 Peter 2:5; Exodus 28:38; Genesis 4:4; Hebrews 11:4.

8 Job 9:20; Psalm 143:2; Philippians 3:12.

9 Hebrews 13:20,21; 2 Corinthians 8:12; Hebrews 6:10; Matthew 25:21,23.

10 2 Kings 10:30,31; 1 Kings 21:27,29; Philippians 1:15,16,18.

use both to themselves and to others:[10] yet because they proceed not from a heart purified by faith;[1] nor are done in a right manner, according to the Word;[2] nor to a right end, the glory of God;[3] they are therefore sinful, and cannot please God, nor make a man meet to receive grace from God;[4] and yet their neglect of them is more sinful, and displeasing unto God.[5]

## *Chapter* 17

# Of the Perseverance of the Saints

1 They whom God hath accepted in his Beloved, effectually called and sanctified by his Spirit, can neither totally nor finally fall away from the state of grace; but shall certainly persevere therein to the end, and be eternally saved.[6]

2 This perseverance of the saints depends not upon their own free will, but upon the immutability of the decree of election; from the free and unchangeable love of God the Father;[7] upon the efficacy of the merit and intercession of Jesus Christ,[8] and union with him;[9] the oath of God;[10] the abiding of his Spirit; and of the seed of God within them;[11] and the nature of the covenant of grace;[12] from all which ariseth also the certainty and infallibility thereof.[13]

3 And though they may, through the temptation of Satan, and of the world, the prevalency of corruption remaining in

---

1 Genesis 4:5; Hebrews 11:4,6.
2 1 Corinthians 13:3; Isaiah 1:12.
3 Matthew 6:2,5,16.
4 Haggai 2:14; Titus 1:15; Amos 5:21,22; Hosea 1:4; Romans 9:16; Titus 3:5.
5 Psalm 14:4; 36:3; Job 21:14,15; Matthew 25:41–43,45; 23:23.
6 Philippians 1:6; 2 Peter 1:10; John 10:28,29; 1 John 3:9; 1 Peter 1:5,9.
7 2 Timothy 2:18,19; Jeremiah 31; 3.

8 Hebrews 10:10,14; 13:20,21; 9:12–15; Romans 8:33–39; John 17:11,24; Luke 22:32.
9 John 17:21.
10 Hebrews 6:17,18; Psalm 89:35,36.
11 John 14:16,17; 1 John 2:27; 3:9.
12 Jeremiah 32:40.
13 John 10:28; 2 Thessalonians 3:3; 1 John 2:19.

them, and the neglect of the means of their preservation, fall into grievous sins;[1] and for a time continue therein,[2] whereby they incur God's displeasure,[3] and grieve his Holy Spirit;[4] come to have their graces and comforts impaired;[5] have their hearts hardened,[6] and their consciences wounded;[7] hurt and scandalize others,[8] and bring temporal judgments upon themselves;[9] yet they are and shall be kept by the power of God through faith unto salvation.[10]

## Chapter 18

# Of the Assurance of Grace and Salvation

1 Although temporary believers and other unregenerate men may vainly deceive themselves with false hopes, and carnal presumptions of being in the favour of God, and state of salvation,[11] which hope of theirs shall perish;[12] yet such as truly believe in the Lord Jesus, and love him in sincerity, endeavouring to walk in all good conscience before him, may in this life be certainly assured that they are in the state of grace,[13] and may rejoice in the hope of the glory of God, which hope shall never make them ashamed.[14]

2 This certainty is not a bare conjectural and probable persuasion, grounded upon a fallible hope;[15] but an infallible assurance of faith, founded on the blood and righteousness of Christ, revealed in the gospel,[16] and also upon the inward evidence of those

1 Matthew 26:70,72,74.
2 Psalm 51:14.
3 Isaiah 64:5,7,9; 2 Samuel 11:27.
4 Ephesians 4:30.
5 Psalm 51:8,10,12; Revelation 2:4; Song of Solomon 5:2–4,6.
6 Isaiah 63:17; Mark 6:52; 16:14.
7 Psalm 32; 3,4; 51:8.
8 2 Samuel 12:14.
9 Psalm 89:31,32; 1 Corinthians 11:30–32.
10 1 Peter 1:5; 1 Thessalonians 5:23.
11 Job 8:13,14; Micah 3:11; Deuteronomy 29:19; John 8:41.
12 Matthew 7:22,23.
13 1 John 2:3; 3:14,18,19,21,24; 5:13.
14 Romans 5:2,5.
15 Hebrews 6:11,19.
16 Hebrews 10:19,20; Romans 3:22.

graces unto which promises are made,[1] and on the immediate witness of the Spirit, testifying our adoption,[2] and as a fruit thereof, leaving the heart more humble and holy.[3]

3 This infallible assurance doth not so belong to the essence of faith, but that a true believer may wait long, and conflict with many difficulties before he be partaker of it;[4] yet being enabled by the Spirit to know the things which are freely given him of God, he may, without extraordinary revelation, in the right use of ordinary means attain thereunto.[5] And therefore it is the duty of every one to give all diligence to make his calling and election sure;[6] that thereby his heart may be enlarged in peace and joy in the Holy Ghost, in love and thankfulness to God, and in strength and cheerfulness in the duties of obedience, the proper fruits of this assurance;[7] so far is it from inclining men to looseness.[8]

4 True believers may have the assurance of their salvation divers ways shaken, diminished and intermitted; as by negligence in preserving of it; by falling into some special sin, which woundeth the conscience, and grieveth the Spirit; by some sudden or vehement temptation; by God's withdrawing the light of his countenance; suffering even such as fear him to walk in darkness, and to have no light;[9] yet are they neither utterly destitute of that seed of God, and life of faith, that love of Christ and the brethren, that sincerity of heart and conscience of duty, out of which by the operation of the Spirit this assurance may

---

1  2 Peter 1:4,5,10,11; 1 John 2:3; 3:14;
   2 Corinthians 1:12.

2  Romans 8:15,16.

3  Psalm 51:12,17; 2 Corinthians 7:1;
   Ephesians 1:13,14; 4:30;
   2 Corinthians 1:21,22.

4  1 John 5:13; Isaiah 50:10; Mark 9:24;
   Psalm 88:1–18; 77:1–12.

5  1 Corinthians 2:12; 1 John 4:13; Hebrews
   6:11,12; Ephesians 3:17–19.

6  2 Peter 2:10.

7  Romans 5:1,2,5; 14:7; 15:13; Ephesians
   1:3,4; Psalm 4:6,7; 119:32.

8  1 John 3:2,3; Psalm 1:3,4; 1 John 2:1,2;
   Romans 6:1,2; Titus 2:11,12,14;
   2 Corinthians 7:1; Romans 8:1,12;
   1 John 1:6,7; Psalm 130:4.

9  Song of Solomon 5:2,3,6; Psalm
   51:8,12,14; Ephesians 4:30,31; Psalm
   77:1–10; Matthew 26:69–72; Psalm
   31:22; 88:1–18; Isaiah 51:10.

in due time be revived,[1] and by the which in the meantime they are supported from utter despair.[2]

## *Chapter* 19

# Of the Law of God

1 God gave to Adam a law of universal obedience written in his heart, and a particular precept of not eating the fruit of the tree of knowledge of good and evil, as a covenant of works, by which he bound him and all his posterity to personal, entire, exact and perpetual obedience; promised life upon the fulfilling, and threatened death upon the breach of it; and endued him with power and ability to keep it.[3]

2 This law, so written in the heart, continued to be a perfect rule of righteousness after the fall of man; and was delivered by God upon mount Sinai in ten commandments, and written in two tables;[4] the four first commandments containing our duty towards God, and the other six our duty to man.[5]

3 Beside this law, commonly called moral, God was pleased to give to the people of Israel ceremonial laws, containing several typical ordinances; partly of worship, prefiguring Christ, his graces, actions, sufferings and benefits,[6] and partly holding forth divers instructions of moral duties.[7] All which ceremonial laws being appointed only to the time of reformation, are by Jesus

---

1  1 John 3:9; Luke 22:32; Job 13:15; Psalm 73:15; 51:8,12; Isaiah 50:10.
2  Micah 7:7–9; Jeremiah 32:40; Isaiah 54:7–10; Psalm 22:1; 88:1–18.
3  Genesis 1:26,27; 2:17; Romans 2:14,15; 10:5; 5:12,19; Galatians 3:10,12; Ecclesiastes 7:29; Job 28:28.
4  James 1:25; 2:8,10–12; Romans 13:8,9; Deuteronomy 5:32; 10:4; Exodus 34:1.
5  Matthew 22:37–40.
6  Hebrews 9; 10:1; Galatians 4:1–3; Colossians 2:17.
7  1 Corinthians 5:7; 2 Corinthians 6:17; Jude 23.

Christ the true Messiah and only lawgiver, who was furnished with power from the Father for that end, abrogated and taken away.[1]

4 To them also he gave sundry judicial laws, which expired together with the state of that people, not obliging any now by virtue of that institution, their general equity only being still of moral use.[2]

5 The moral law doth for ever bind all, as well justified persons as others, to the obedience thereof;[3] and that not only in regard of the matter contained in it,[4] but also in respect of the authority of God the Creator, who gave it: neither doth Christ in the gospel any way dissolve, but much strengthen this obligation.[5]

6 Although true believers be not under the law, as a covenant of works, to be thereby justified or condemned;[6] yet it is of great use to them as well as to others, in that, as a rule of life, informing them of the will of God, and their duty, it directs and binds them to walk accordingly;[7] discovering also the sinful pollutions of their nature, hearts and lives;[8] so as examining themselves thereby, they may come to further conviction of, humiliation for, and hatred against sin;[9] together with a clearer sight of the need they have of Christ, and the perfection of his obedience.[10] It is likewise of use to the regenerate, to restrain their corruptions, in that it forbids sin;[11] and the threatenings of it serve to show what even their sins deserve, and what afflictions in this life they may expect for them, although freed from the curse thereof

---

1 Hebrews 9:10,11; James 4:12; Hebrews 7:12; Colossians 2:14,16,17; Ephesians 2:15,16.

2 Exodus 21; 22:1–29; Genesis 49:10; 1 Peter 2:13,14; Matthew 5:17,38,39.

3 Romans 13:8–10; Ephesians 6:1,2,6; 1 John 2:3,4,7,8.

4 James 2:10,11.

5 Matthew 5:17–19; James 2:8; Romans 3:31.

6 Romans 6:14; Galatians 2:16; 3:13; 4:4,5; Acts 13:39; Romans 8:1.

7 Romans 7:12,22,25; Psalm 119:4–6; 1 Corinthians 7:19; Galatians 5:14,16,18–23.

8 Romans 7:7; 3:20.

9 James 1:23–25; Romans 7:9,14,24.

10 Galatians 3:24; Romans 7:24,25; 8:3,4.

11 James 2:11; Psalm 119:101,104,128.

threatened in the law.[1] The promises of it in like manner show them God's approbation of obedience, and what blessings they may expect upon the performance thereof,[2] although not as due to them by the law, as a covenant of works;[3] so as a mans doing good, and refraining from evil, because the law encourageth to the one, and deterreth from the other, is no evidence of his being under the law, and not under grace.[4]

7 Neither are the forementioned uses of the law contrary to the grace of the gospel, but do sweetly comply with it;[5] the Spirit of Christ subduing and enabling the will of man to do that freely and cheerfully, which the will of God revealed in the law required to be done.[6]

## Chapter 20

# Of the Gospel, and of the extent of the Grace thereof

1 The covenant of works being broken by sin, and made unprofitable unto life,[7] God was pleased to give unto the elect the promise of Christ, the seed of the woman,[8] as the means of calling them, and begetting in them faith and repentance:[9] in this promise the gospel, as to the substance of it, was revealed, and was therein effectual for the conversion and salvation of sinners.[10]

---

1 Ezra 9:13,14; Psalm 89:30–35.
2 Leviticus 26:1–14; 2 Corinthians 6:16; Ephesians 6:2,3; Psalm 37:11; Matthew 5:5; Psalm 19:11.
3 Galatians 2:16; Luke 17:10.
4 Romans 6:12,14; 1 Peter 3:8–12; Psalm 34:12–16; Hebrews 12:28,29.
5 Galatians 3:21.
6 Ezekiel 36:26,27; Hebrews 8:10; Jeremiah 31:33.
7 Romans 8:3; Galatians 3:12.
8 Genesis 3:15; Galatians 4:4,5; Revelation 13:3.
9 1 Corinthians 1:23,24,26; James 1:18; Romans 10:8; Acts 11:15,18.
10 1 Corinthians 2:2.

2 This promise of Christ, and salvation by him, is revealed only in and by the Word of God;[1] neither do the works of creation or providence, with the light of nature, make discovery of Christ, or of grace by him, so much as in a general or obscure way;[2] much less that men destitute of the revelation of him by the promise or gospel, should be enabled thereby to attain saving faith or repentance.[3]

3 The revelation of the gospel unto sinners, made in divers times, and by sundry parts, with the addition of promises and precepts for the obedience required therein, as to the nations and persons to whom it is granted, is merely of the sovereign will and good pleasure of God,[4] not being annexed by virtue of any promise to the due improvement of men's natural abilities, by virtue of common light received without it, which none ever did make or can so do.[5] And therefore in all ages the preaching of the gospel hath been granted unto persons and nations, as to the extent or straitening of it, in great variety, according to the counsel of the will of God.[6]

4 Although the gospel be the only outward means of revealing Christ and saving grace, and is as such abundantly sufficient thereunto; yet that men who are dead in trespasses, may be born again, quickened or regenerated, there is moreover necessary an effectual, irresistible work of the Holy Ghost upon the whole soul, for the producing in them a new spiritual life, without which no other means are sufficient for their conversion unto God.[7]

---

1 Matthew 11:27; 2 Timothy 1:10.

2 Romans 1:19,20; Ephesians 2:12; Romans 16:25,26; Ephesians 3:9.

3 1 Corinthians 1:21; Romans 10:14,15; Proverbs 29:18.

4 Hebrews 1:1,2; Deuteronomy 7:7,8; Psalm 147:19,20; Matthew 21:43; 11:25,26.

5 John 1:13; 3:6; Romans 9:16; Philippians 2:13; John 15:5; 1 Corinthians 2:14; Romans 8:7.

6 Amos 3:2; Matthew 28:19; 21:43; Ephesians 1:11.

7 Ephesians 2:1,5; Titus 3:5; John 16:7–12; Acts 16:14; Ephesians 1:19,20; 1 Thessalonians 5:23; John 3:6; Galatians 2:8.

## Chapter 21

# Of Christian Liberty, and Liberty of Conscience

1 The liberty which Christ hath purchased for believers under the gospel, consists in their freedom from the guilt of sin, the condemning wrath of God, the rigour and curse of the law;[1] and in their being delivered from this present evil world, bondage to Satan, and dominion of sin,[2] from the evil of afflictions, the fear and sting of death, the victory of the grave, and everlasting damnation;[3] as also in their free access to God,[4] and their yielding obedience unto him, not out of slavish fear, but a childlike love and willing mind.[5] All which were common also to believers under the law, for the substance of them;[6] but under the New Testament the liberty of Christians is further enlarged in their freedom from the yoke of the ceremonial law, the whole legal administration of the covenant of grace, to which the Jewish church was subjected;[7] and in greater boldness of access to the throne of grace,[8] and in fuller communications of the free Spirit of God, than believers under the law did ordinarily partake of.[9]

2 God alone is lord of the conscience,[10] and hath left it free from the doctrines and commandments of men which are in any thing contrary to his Word, or not contained in it;[11] so that to believe such doctrines, or to obey such commands out of conscience, is to betray true liberty of conscience;[12] and the

---

1 Titus 2:14; 1 Thessalonians 1:10; Galatians 3:13.
2 Galatians 1:4; Colossians 1:13; Acts 26:18; Romans 6:14.
3 Romans 8:28; Psalm 119:71; 1 Corinthians 15:54–57; Romans 8:1.
4 Romans 5:1,2.
5 Romans 8:14,15; 1 John 4:18.
6 Galatians 3:9,13,14.

7 Galatians 4:1–3,6,7; 5:1; Acts 15:10,11.
8 Hebrews 4:14,16; 10:19–22.
9 John 7:38,39; 2 Corinthians 3:13,17,18.
10 James 4:12; Romans 14:4.
11 Acts 4:19; 5:29; 1 Corinthians 7:23; Matthew 23:8–10; 2 Corinthians 1:24; Matthew 15:9.
12 Colossians 2:20,22,23; Galatians 1:10; 2:2,4,5; 5:1.

requiring of an implicit faith, and an absolute and blind obedience, is to destroy liberty of conscience, and reason also.[1]

3 They who upon pretence of Christian liberty do practise any sin, or cherish any lust, as they do thereby pervert the main design of the grace of the gospel to their own destruction; so they wholly destroy the end of Christian liberty, which is, that being delivered out of the hands of our enemies, we might serve the Lord without fear, in holiness and righteousness before him all the days of our life.[2]

## Chapter 22

# Of religious Worship, and the Sabbath-day

1 The light of nature showeth that there is a God, who hath lordship and sovereignty over all, is just, good, and doth good unto all, and is therefore to be feared, loved, praised, called upon, trusted in, and served with all the heart, and all the soul, and with all the might.[3] But the acceptable way of worshipping the true God is instituted by himself, and so limited by his own revealed will, that he may not be worshipped according to the imaginations and devices of men, or the suggestions of Satan, under any visible representations, or any other way not prescribed in the holy Scripture.[4]

---

1 Romans 10:17; 14:23; Isaiah 8:20; Acts 17:11; John 4:22; Hosea 5:11; Jeremiah 8:9; Revelation 13:12.
2 Galatians 5:13; 1 Peter 2:16; 2 Peter 2:19; John 8:34; Luke 1:74,75.

3 Romans 1:20; Acts 17:24; Psalm 119:68; Jeremiah 10:7; Psalm 31:23; 18:3; Romans 10:12; Psalm 62:8; Josh. 24:14; Mark 12:33.
4 Deuteronomy 12:32; Matthew 15:9; Acts 17:25; Matthew 4:9,10; Deuteronomy 4:1–20; Exodus 20:4,5.

2 Religious worship is to be given to God the Father, Son, and Holy Ghost, and to him alone;[1] not to angels, saints, or any other creatures;[2] and since the fall, not without a Mediator, nor in the mediation of any other but of Christ alone.[3]

3 Prayer, with thanksgiving, being one special part of natural worship,[4] is by God required of all men;[5] but that it may be accepted, it is to be made in the name of the Son[6] by the help of his Spirit,[7] according to his will,[8] with understanding, reverence, humility, fervency, faith, love, and perseverance;[9] and when with others in a known tongue.[10]

4 Prayer is to be made for things lawful,[11] and for all sorts of men living, or that shall live hereafter;[12] but not for the dead,[13] nor for those of whom it may be known that they have sinned the sin unto death.[14]

5 The reading of the Scriptures,[15] preaching,[16] and hearing the Word of God,[17] singing of psalms;[18] as also the administration of baptism and the Lord's Supper, are all parts of religious worship of God, to be performed in obedience unto God with understanding, faith, reverence, and godly fear.[19] Solemn humiliations, with fastings[20] and thanksgivings upon special

---

1 Matthew 4:10; John 5:23; 2 Corinthians 13:14.

2 Colossians 2:18; Revelation 19:10; Romans 1:25.

3 John 14:6; 1 Timothy 2:5; Ephesians 2:18; Colossians 3:17.

4 Philippians 4:6.

5 Psalm 65:2.

6 John 14:13,14; 1 Peter 2:5.

7 Romans 8:26.

8 1 John 5:14.

9 Psalm 47:7; Ecclesiastes 5:1,2; Hebrews 12:28; Genesis 18:27; James 5:16; Mark 11:24; Matthew 6:12,14,15; Colossians 4:2; Ephesians 6:18; James 1:6–7.

10 1 Corinthians 14:14.

11 1 John 5:14.

12 1 Timothy 2:1,2; John 17:20; 2 Samuel 7:29; Ruth 4:12.

13 2 Samuel 12:21–23; Luke 16:25,26; Revelation 14:13.

14 1 John 5:16.

15 Acts 15:21; Revelation 1:3.

16 2 Timothy 4:2.

17 James 1:21,22; Acts 10:33; Matthew 13:19; Hebrews 4:2; Isaiah 66:2.

18 Colossians 3:16; Ephesians 5:19; James 5:13.

19 Matthew 28:19; 1 Corinthians 11:23–29; Acts 2:41,42.

20 Joel 2:12; Esther 4:16; Matthew 9:15; 1 Corinthians 7:5.

occasions,[1] are in their several times and seasons to be used in a holy and religious manner.[2]

6 Neither prayer, nor any other part of religious worship, is now under the gospel either tied unto, or made more acceptable by any place in which it is performed, or towards which it is directed;[3] but God is to be worshipped everywhere[4] in spirit and in truth,[5] as in private families[6] daily,[7] and in secret each one by himself,[8] so more solemnly in the public assemblies, which are not carelessly nor wilfully to be neglected, or forsaken, when God by his Word or providence calleth thereunto.[9]

7 As it is of the law of nature, that in general a proportion of time by God's appointment be set apart for the worship of God; so by his Word in a positive, moral, and perpetual commandment, binding all men in all ages, he hath particularly appointed one day in seven for a Sabbath to be kept holy unto him;[10] which from the beginning of the world to the resurrection of Christ, was the last day of the week; and from the resurrection of Christ was changed into the first day of the week,[11] which in Scripture is called the Lord's Day,[12] and is to be continued to the end of the world as the Christian Sabbath, the observation of the last day of the week being abolished.[13]

8 This Sabbath is then kept holy unto the Lord, when men after a due preparing of their hearts, and ordering their common affairs beforehand, do not only observe an holy rest all the day from their own works, words, and thoughts about their worldly

---

1 Psalm 107:1–43; Esther 9:22.
2 Hebrews 12:28.
3 John 4:21.
4 Malachi 1:11; 1 Timothy 2:8.
5 John 4:23,24.
6 Jeremiah 10:25; Deuteronomy 6:6,7; Job 1:5; 2 Samuel 6:18,20; 1 Peter 3:7; Acts 10:2.
7 Matthew 6:11.
8 Matthew 6:6; Ephesians 6:18.

9 Isaiah 56:6,7; Hebrews 10:25; Proverbs 1:20,21,24; 8:34; Acts 13:42; Luke 4:16; Acts 2:42.
10 Exodus 20:8–11; Isaiah 56:2–7.
11 Genesis 2:2,3; 1 Corinthians 16:1,2; Acts 20:7.
12 Revelation 1:10.
13 Exodus 20:8,10; Matthew 5:17,18.

employments and recreations;[1] but also are taken up the whole time in the public and private exercises of his worship, and in the duties of necessity and mercy.[2]

## *Chapter* 23

# Of Lawful Oaths and Vows

1 A lawful oath is a part of religious worship,[3] wherein the person swearing in truth, righteousness and judgment, solemnly calleth God to witness what he asserteth or promiseth, and to judge him according to the truth or falsehood of what he sweareth.[4]

2 The name of God only is that by which men ought to swear, and therein it is to be used with all holy fear and reverence.[5] Therefore to swear vainly, or rashly, by that glorious or dreadful name, or to swear at all by any other thing, is sinful and to be abhorred.[6] Yet as in matters of weight and moment an oath is warranted by the Word of God under the New Testament, as well as under the Old;[7] so a lawful oath, being imposed by lawful authority in such matters, ought to be taken.[8]

3 Whosoever taketh an oath, warranted by the Word of God, ought duly to consider the weightiness of so solemn an act, and therein to avouch nothing but what he is fully persuaded is the truth:[9] neither may any man bind himself by oath to any thing, but what is good and just, and what he believeth so to be, and

---

1 Exodus 20:8; 16:23–30; 31:15–17; Isaiah 58:13; Nehemiah 13:15–23.
2 Isaiah 58:13; Matthew 12:1–14.
3 Deuteronomy 10:20.
4 Jeremiah 4:2; Exodus 20:7; Leviticus 19:12; 2 Corinthians 1:23; 2 Chronicles 6:22,23.
5 Deuteronomy 6:13.
6 Exodus 20:7; Jeremiah 5:7; Matthew 5:34–37; James 5:12.
7 Hebrews 6:16; 2 Corinthians 1:23; Isaiah 65:16.
8 1 Kings 8:31; Nehemiah 13:25; Ezra 10:5.
9 Exodus 20:7; Jeremiah 4:2.

what he is able and resolved to perform.[1] Yet it is a sin to refuse an oath touching any thing that is good and just, being lawfully imposed by authority.[2]

4 An oath is to be taken in the plain and common sense of the words, without equivocation or mental reservation.[3] It cannot oblige to sin, but in any thing not sinful, being taken it binds to performance, although to a man's own hurt;[4] nor is it to be violated, although made to heretics or infidels.[5]

5 A vow, which is not to be made to any creature, but God alone, is of the like nature with a promissory oath, and ought to be made with the like religious care, and to be performed with the like faithfulness.[6]

6 Popish monastical vows of perpetual single life, professed poverty, and regular obedience, are so far from being degrees of higher perfection, that they are superstitious and sinful snares, in which no Christian may entangle himself.[7]

## Chapter 24

# Of the Civil Magistrate

1 God the supreme Lord and King of all the world, hath ordained civil magistrates to be under him, over the people for his own glory and the public good; and to this end hath armed them with the power of the sword, for the defence and encouragement of them that do good, and for the punishment of evil-doers.[8]

---

1 Genesis 24:1–3,5,6,8,9.
2 Numbers 5:19,21; Nehemiah 5:12; Exodus 22:7–11.
3 Jeremiah 4:2; Psalm 24:4.
4 1 Samuel 25:22,31–34; Psalm 15:4.
5 Ezekiel 17:16,18,19; Josh. 9:18,19; 2 Samuel 21:1.

6 Psalm 76:11; Jeremiah 44:25,26; Psalm 50:14; 65:1; Isaiah 19:21; Ecclesiastes 5:4–6; Psalm 61:8; 66:13,14.
7 Matthew 19:11,12; 1 Corinthians 7:2,9; Ephesians 4:28; 1 Peter 4:2; 1 Corinthians 7:23.
8 Romans 13:1–4; 1 Peter 2:13,14.

2 It is lawful for Christians to accept and execute the office of a magistrate, when called thereunto:[1] in the management whereof, as they ought specially to maintain justice and peace, according to the wholesome laws of each commonwealth;[2] so for that end they may lawfully now under the New Testament wage war upon just and necessary occasion.[3]

3 Although the magistrate is bound to encourage, promote, and protect the professors and profession of the gospel, and to manage and order civil administrations in a due subserviency to the interest of Christ in the world, and to that end to take care that men of corrupt minds and conversations do not licentiously publish and divulge blasphemy and errors, in their own nature subverting the faith and inevitably destroying the souls of them that receive them: yet in such differences about the doctrines of the gospel, or ways of the worship of God, as may befall men exercising a good conscience, manifesting it in their conversation, and holding the foundation, not disturbing others in their ways or worship that differ from them; there is no warrant for the magistrate under the gospel to abridge them of their liberty.[4]

4 It is the duty of people to pray for magistrates, to honour their persons, to pay them tribute and other dues, to obey their lawful commands, and to be subject to their authority for conscience sake. Infidelity, or difference in religion, doth not make void the magistrate's just and legal authority, nor free the people from their obedience to him: from which ecclesiastical persons are not exempted, much less hath the Pope any power or jurisdiction over them in their dominions, or over any of their people, and least of all to deprive them of their dominions

---

1 Proverbs 8:15,16; Romans 13:1,2,4.
2 Psalm 2:10–12; 1 Timothy 2:2; Psalm 82:3,4; 2 Samuel 23:3; 1 Peter 2:13.

3 Luke 3:14; Romans 13:4; Matthew 8:9,10; Acts 10:1,2; Revelation 17:14,16.
4 Romans 13:1–4.

or lives, if he shall judge them to be heretics, or upon any other pretence whatsoever.[1]

## Chapter 25

# Of Marriage

1 Marriage is to be between one man and one woman: neither is it lawful for any man to have more than one wife, nor for any woman to have more than one husband at the same time.[2]

2 Marriage was ordained for the mutual help of husband and wife;[3] for the increase of mankind with a legitimate issue, and of the Church with an holy seed,[4] and for preventing of uncleanness.[5]

3 It is lawful for all sorts of people to marry, who are able with judgment to give their consent.[6] Yet it is the duty of Christians to marry in the Lord;[7] and therefore such as profess the true reformed religion, should not marry with infidels, Papists, or other idolaters: neither should such as are godly, be unequally yoked by marrying with such as are wicked in their life, or maintain damnable heresies.[8]

4 Marriage ought not to be within the degrees of consanguity or affinity forbidden in the Word;[9] nor can such incestuous marriages ever be made lawful by any law of man, or consent of parties, so as those persons may live together as man and wife.[10]

---

1  1 Timothy 2:1,2; 1 Peter 2:17; Romans 13:5–7; Titus 3:1; 1 Peter 2:13,14,16; Romans 13:1; 1 Kings 2:35; Acts 25:9–11; 2 Peter 2:1,10,11; Jude 8–11; 2 Thessalonians 2:4; Revelation 13:15–17.
2  Genesis 2:24; Matthew 19:5,6; Proverbs 2:17.
3  Genesis 2:18.
4  Malachi 2:15.
5  1 Corinthians 7:2,9.

6  Hebrews 13:4; 1 Timothy 4:3; 1 Corinthians 7: 36–38; Genesis 24:57,58.
7  1 Corinthians 7:39.
8  Genesis 34:14; Exodus 34:16; Deuteronomy 7:3,4; 1 Kings 11:4; Nehemiah 13:25–27; Mal. 2:11,12; 2 Corinthians 6:14.
9  Leviticus 18:1–30; 1 Corinthians 5:1; Amos 2:7.
10 Mark 6:18; Leviticus 18:24–29.

## Chapter 26

# Of the Church

1 The catholic or universal church, which is invisible, consists of the whole number of the elect, that have been, are, or shall be gathered into one under Christ, the Head thereof, and is the Spouse, the Body, the fullness of him that filleth all in all.[1]

2 The whole body of men throughout the world, professing the faith of the gospel and obedience unto God by Christ according to it,[2] not destroying their own profession by any errors everting the foundation,[3] or unholiness of conversation,[4] are, and may be called the visible catholic church of Christ;[5] although as such it is not entrusted with the administration of any ordinances, or have any officers to rule or govern in, or over the whole body.[6]

3 The purest churches under heaven are subject both to mixture and error,[7] and some have so degenerated as to become no churches of Christ, but synagogues of Satan:[8] nevertheless Christ always hath had, and ever shall have, a visible kingdom in this world, to the end thereof, of such as believe in him, and make profession of his name.[9]

4 There is no other Head of the Church but the Lord Jesus Christ;[10] nor can the Pope of Rome in any sense be head thereof; but is that antichrist, that man of sin, and son of perdition, that exalteth himself in the Church against Christ, and all that is

---

1 Ephesians 1:10,22,23; 5:23,27,32; Colossians 1:18.
2 1 Corinthians 1:2; Colossians 2:19.
3 1 Timothy 1:19,20.
4 2 Timothy 2:19; Titus 1:16; 1 Corinthians 7:14; Acts 2:39; Ezekiel 16:20,21; Romans 11:16; Genesis 3:15; 17:7.
5 1 Corinthians 12:12,13; Romans 15:9,10,12.

6 Ephesians 4:8,11,12; Romans 12:6–8; 1 Corinthians 12:28–30.
7 1 Corinthians 13:12; Revelation 2:1–29; 3:1–22; Matthew 13:24–30,47.
8 Revelation 18:2; Romans 11:18–23.
9 Matthew 16:18; Psalm 72:17; 102:28; Matt 28:19,20.
10 Colossians 1:18; Ephesians 1:22.

called God, whom the Lord shall destroy with the brightness of his coming.[1]

5 As the Lord in his care and love towards his Church, hath in his infinite wise providence exercised it with great variety in all ages, for the good of them that love him, and his own glory;[2] so according to his promise, we expect that in the latter days, antichrist being destroyed,[3] the Jews called,[4] and the adversaries of the kingdom of his dear Son broken,[5] the churches of Christ being enlarged, and edified through a free and plentiful communication of light and grace, shall enjoy in this world a more quiet, peaceable and glorious condition than they have enjoyed.[6]

## Chapter 27

# Of the Communion of Saints

1 All Saints that are united to Jesus Christ their Head, by his Spirit and faith, although they are not made thereby one person with him,[7] have fellowship in his graces, sufferings, death, resurrection and glory:[8] and being united to one another in love, they have communion in each others gifts and graces,[9] and are obliged to the performance of such duties, public and private, as do conduce to their mutual good, both in the inward and outward man.[10]

---

1 Matthew 23:8–10; 2 Thessalonians 2:3,4,8,9; Revelation 13:6.

2 Acts 7:1–51; 14:22; 8:1; 9:31.

3 2 Thessalonians 2:8–10; Revelation 18:2,4,21; 17:16.

4 Romans 10:1; 11:23–32.

5 Psalm 110:1; 2:9.

6 Isaiah 11:9; Joel 2:28,29; Isaiah 2:2–4; Micah 4:3; Psalm 87:2–7; Daniel 7:27.

7 Colossians 1:18,19; 1 Corinthians 8:6; Isaiah 42:8; 1 Timothy 6:15,16; Psalm 45:7; Hebrews 1:8,9.

8 1 John 1:3; Ephesians 3:16–19; John 1:16; Ephesians 2:5,6; Philippians 3:10; Romans 6:5,6; 2 Timothy 2:12.

9 Ephesians 4:15,16; 1 Corinthians 12:7; 3:21–23; Colossians 2:19.

10 1 Thessalonians 5:11,14; Romans 1:11,12,14; 1 John 3:16–18; Galatians 6:10.

2 All saints are bound to maintain an holy fellowship and communion in the worship of God, and in performing such other spiritual services as tend to their mutual edification;[1] as also in relieving each other in outward things, according to their several abilities and necessities: which communion, though especially to be exercised by them in the relations wherein they stand, whether in families[2] or churches, yet as God offereth opportunity, is to be extended unto all those who in every place call upon the Name of the Lord Jesus.[3]

## Chapter 28

# Of the Sacraments

1 Sacraments are holy signs and seals of the covenant of grace,[4] immediately instituted by Christ,[5] to represent him and his benefits, and to confirm our interest in him,[6] and solemnly to engage us to the service of God in Christ, according to his Word.[7]

2 There is in every sacrament a spiritual relation, or sacramental union, between the sign and the thing signified; whence it comes to pass that the names and effects of the one are attributed to the other.[8]

3 The grace which is exhibited in or by the sacraments rightly used, is not conferred by any power in them; neither doth the efficacy of a sacrament depend upon the piety or intention of him that doth administer it,[9] but upon the work of the Spirit,[10] and the word of institution; which contains, together with a

---

1 Hebrews 10:24,25; Acts 2:42,46; Isaiah 2:3; 1 Corinthians 11:20.
2 Ephesians 6:2,4,5,9; 5:22–26; 1 Timothy 5:8; Galatians 6:10.
3 Acts 2:44,45; 1 John 3:17; 2 Corinthians 8:1–24; 9:1–15; Acts 11:29,30.
4 Romans 4:11; Genesis 17:7,10.
5 Matthew 28:19; 1 Corinthians 11:23.
6 1 Corinthians 10:16; 11:25,26.
7 Romans 6:3,4; 1 Corinthians 10:16,21.
8 Genesis 17:10; Matthew 26:27,28; Titus 3:5.
9 Romans 2:28,29; 1 Peter 3:21.
10 Matthew 3:11; 1 Corinthians 12:13.

precept authorising the use thereof, a promise of benefit to worthy receivers.[1]

4 There be only two sacraments ordained by Christ our Lord in the gospel, that is to say, Baptism and the Lord's Supper; neither of which may be dispensed by any but a minister of the Word lawfully called.[2]

5 The Sacraments of the Old Testament, in regard of the spiritual things thereby signified and exhibited, were for substance the same with those of the New.[3]

## *Chapter* 29

# Of Baptism

1 Baptism is a sacrament of the New Testament, ordained by Jesus Christ[4] to be unto the party baptised a sign and seal of the covenant of grace,[5] of his ingrafting into Christ,[6] of regeneration,[7] of remission of sins,[8] and of his giving up unto God through Jesus Christ to walk in newness of life;[9] which ordinance is by Christ's own appointment to be continued in his Church until the end of the world.[10]

2 The outward element to be used in this ordinance, is water, wherewith the party is to be baptised in the name of the Father, and of the Son, and of the Holy Ghost, by a minister of the gospel lawfully called.[11]

---

1 Matthew 26:27,28; 28:19,20
2 Matthew 28:19; 1 Corinthians 11:20,23; 4:1; Hebrews 5:4.
3 1 Corinthians 10:1–4.
4 Matthew 28:19.
5 Romans 4:11; Colossians 2:11,12.
6 Galatians 3:27; Romans 6:5.
7 Titus 3:5.
8 Mark 1:4.
9 Romans 6:3,4.
10 Matthew 28:19,20.
11 Matthew 3:11; John 1:33; Matthew 28:19,20.

3 Dipping of the person into the water is not necessary; but baptism is rightly administered by pouring or sprinkling water upon the person.[1]

4 Not only those that do actually profess faith in and obedience unto Christ,[2] but also the infants of one or both believing parents are to be baptised, and those only.[3]

5 Although it be a great sin to contemn or neglect this ordinance,[4] yet grace and salvation are not so inseparably annexed unto it,[5] as that no person can be regenerated or saved without it; or that all that are baptised are undoubtedly regenerated.[6]

6 The efficacy of baptism is not tied to that moment of time wherein it is administered;[7] yet notwithstanding, by the right use of this ordinance, the grace promised is not only offered, but really exhibited and conferred by the Holy Ghost to such (whether of age or infants) as that grace belongeth unto, according to the counsel of God's own will in his appointed time.[8]

7 Baptism is but once to be administered to any person.[9]

## Chapter 30

# Of the Lord's Supper

1 Our Lord Jesus in the night wherein he was betrayed, instituted the sacrament of his body and blood, called the Lord's Supper, to be observed in his churches to the end of the world, for the perpetual remembrance, and showing forth of the sacrifice of himself in his death, the sealing of all benefits thereof unto

---

1 Hebrews 9:10,19–22; Acts 2:41; 16:33; Mark 7:4.
2 Mark 16:15,16; Acts 8: 37,38.
3 Genesis 17:7,9; Galatians 3:9,14; Colossians 2:11; Acts 2:38,39; Romans 4:11,12; 1 Corinthians 7:14; Matthew 28:19; Mark 10:13–16; Luke 18:15.

4 Luke 7:30; Exodus 4:24–26.
5 Romans 4:11; Acts 10:2,4,22,31,45,47.
6 Acts 8:13,23.
7 John 3:5,8.
8 Galatians 3:27; Titus 3:5; Ephesians 5:25,26; Acts 2:38,41.
9 Titus 3:5.

true believers, their spiritual nourishment, and growth in him, their further engagement in and to all duties which they owe unto him, and to be a bond and pledge of their communion with him, and with each other.[1]

2 In this sacrament Christ is not offered up to his Father, nor any real sacrifice made at all for remission of sin of the quick or dead,[2] but only a memorial of that one offering up of himself upon the cross once for all, and a spiritual oblation of all possible praise unto God for the same;[3] so that the Popish sacrifice of the mass (as they call it) is most abominable, injurious to Christ's own only sacrifice, the alone propitiation for all the sins of the elect.[4]

3 The Lord Jesus hath in this ordinance appointed his ministers to pray and bless the elements of bread and wine, and thereby to set them apart from a common to an holy use; and to take and break the bread, to take the cup, and (they communicating also themselves) to give both to the communicants;[5] but to none who are not then present in the congregation.[6]

4 Private masses, or receiving the sacrament by a priest, or any other, alone;[7] as likewise the denial of the cup to the people;[8] worshipping the elements, the lifting them up, or carrying them about for adoration, and the reserving them for any pretended religious use; are contrary to the nature of this sacrament, and to the institution of Christ.[9]

5 The outward elements in this sacrament duly set apart to the uses ordained by Christ, have such relation to him crucified, as that truly, yet sacramentally only, they are sometimes called by the name of the things they represent, to wit, the body and

---

1 1 Corinthians 11:23–26; 10:16,17,21; 12:13.
2 Hebrews 9:22,25,26,28.
3 1 Corinthians 11: 24–26; Matthew 26:26,27.
4 Hebrews 7:23,24,27; 10:11,12,14,18.

5 Matthew 26:26–28; Mark 14:22–24; Luke 22:19,20; 1 Corinthians 11:23–26.
6 Acts 20:7; 1 Corinthians 11:20.
7 1 Corinthians 10:6.
8 Mark 14:23; 1 Corinthians 11:25–30.
9 Matthew 15:9.

blood of Christ;[1] albeit, in substance and nature, they still remain truly and only bread and wine as they were before.[2]

6 The doctrine which maintains a change of the substance of bread and wine into the substance of Christ's body and blood (commonly called transubstantiation) by consecration of a priest, or by any other way, is repugnant not to Scripture alone, but even to common sense and reason; overthroweth the nature of the sacrament; and hath been and is the cause of manifold superstitions, yea, of gross idolatries.[3]

7 Worthy receivers outwardly partaking of the visible elements in this sacrament,[4] do then also inwardly by faith, really and indeed, yet not carnally and corporally, but spiritually, receive and feed upon Christ crucified, and all benefits of his death; the body and blood of Christ being then not corporally or carnally in, with, or under the bread or wine; yet as really, but spiritually present to the faith of believers in that ordinance, as the elements themselves are to their outward senses.[5]

8 All ignorant and ungodly persons, as they are unfit to enjoy communion with Christ, so are they unworthy of the Lord's table, and cannot without great sin against him, while they remain such, partake of these holy mysteries,[6] or be admitted thereunto;[7] yea, whosoever shall receive unworthily, are guilty of the body and blood of the Lord, eating and drinking judgment to themselves.[8]

---

1 Matthew 26:26–28.
2 1 Corinthians 11:26–28; Matthew 26:29.
3 Acts 3:21; 1 Corinthians 11:24–26; Luke 24:6,39.
4 1 Corinthians 11:28.
5 1 Corinthians 10:16.
6 1 Corinthians 11:27–29; 2 Corinthians 6:14–16.
7 1 Corinthians 5:6,7,13; 2 Thessalonians 3:6,14,15; Matthew 7:6.
8 1 Corinthians 11:27,29.

## Chapter 31

# Of the state of Man after Death, and of the Resurrection of the Dead

1 The bodies of men after death return to dust, and see corruption;[1] but their souls (which neither die nor sleep) having an immortal subsistence, immediately return to God who gave them.[2] The souls of the righteous being then made perfect in holiness, are received into the highest heavens, where they behold the face of God in light and glory, waiting for the full redemption of their bodies:[3] and the souls of the wicked are cast into hell, where they remain in torment and utter darkness, reserved to the judgment of the great day:[4] Besides these two places for souls separated from their bodies, the Scripture acknowledgeth none.

2 At the last day such as are found alive shall not die, but be changed;[5] and all the dead shall be raised up with the self-same bodies, and none other, although with different qualities, which shall be united again to their souls for ever.[6]

3 The bodies of the unjust shall by the power of Christ be raised to dishonour; the bodies of the just, by his Spirit unto honour, and to be made conformable to his own glorious body.[7]

---

1 Genesis 3:19; Acts 13:36.
2 Luke 23:43; Ecclesiastes 12:7.
3 Hebrews 12:23; 2 Corinthians 5:1,6,8; Philippians 1:23; Acts 3:21; Ephesians 4:10.
4 Luke 16:23,24; Acts 1:25; Jude 5–7; 1 Peter 3:19.
5 1 Thessalonians 4:17; 1 Corinthians 15:51,52.
6 Job 19:25–27; 1 Corinthians 15:42–44.
7 Acts 24:15; John 5:28,29; 1 Corinthians 15:42–43; Philippians 3:21.

## *Chapter* 32

# Of the last Judgment

1 God hath appointed a day wherein he will judge the world in righteousness by Jesus Christ,[1] to whom all power and judgment is given of the Father.[2] In which day, not only the apostate angels shall be judged,[3] but likewise all persons that have lived upon earth shall appear before the tribunal of Christ, to give an account of their thoughts, words and deeds, and to receive according to what they have done in the body, whether good or evil.[4]

2 The end of God's appointing this day is for the manifestation of the glory of his mercy in the eternal salvation of the elect, and of his justice in the damnation of the reprobate, who are wicked and disobedient. For then shall the righteous go into everlasting life, and receive that fulness of joy and glory, with everlasting reward in the presence of the Lord; but the wicked who know not God, and obey not the gospel of Jesus Christ, shall be cast into eternal torments, and be punished with everlasting destruction from the presence of the Lord, and from the glory of his power.[5]

3 As Christ would have us to be certainly persuaded that there shall be a judgment, both to deter all men from sin, and for the greater consolation of the godly in their adversity;[6] so will he have that day unknown to men, that they may shake off all carnal security, and be always watchful, because they know not at what hour the Lord will come, and may be ever prepared to say, Come Lord Jesus, come quickly,[7] Amen.

---

1 Acts 17:31.

2 John 5:22,27.

3 1 Corinthians 6:3; Jude 5,6; 2 Peter 2:4.

4 2 Corinthians 5:10; Ecclesiastes 12:14; Romans 2:16; 14:10,12; Matthew 12:36,37.

5 Matthew 25:31–46; Romans 2:5,6: 9:22,23; Matthew 25:21; Acts 3:19; 2 Thessalonians 1:7–10.

6 2 Peter 3:11,14; 2 Corinthians 5:10,11; 2 Thessalonians 1:5–7; Luke 21:27,28; Romans 8:23–25.

7 Matthew 24:36,42–44; Mark 13:35–37; Luke 12:35,36; Revelation 22:20.

# The
# Institution of Churches,
### and the
# Order Appointed in Them
### by
# Jesus Christ

1 By the appointment of the Father all power for the calling, institution, order, or government of the Church, is invested in a supreme and sovereign manner in the Lord Jesus Christ, as King and Head thereof.

2 In the execution of this power wherewith he is so entrusted, the Lord Jesus calleth out of the world unto communion with himself, those that are given unto him by his Father, that they may walk before him in all the ways of obedience, which he prescribeth to them in his Word.

3 Those thus called (through the ministry of the Word by his Spirit) he commandeth to walk together in particular societies or churches, for their mutual edification, and the due performance of that public worship, which he requireth of them in this world.

4 To each of these churches thus gathered, according to his mind declared in his Word, he hath given all that power and

authority, which is any way needful for their carrying on that order in worship and discipline, which he hath instituted for them to observe, with commands and rules for the due and right exerting and executing of that power.

5 These particular churches thus appointed by the authority of Christ, and entrusted with power from him for the ends before expressed, are each of them as unto those ends, the seat of that power which he is pleased to communicate to his saints or subjects in this world, so that as such they receive it immediately from himself.

6 Besides these particular churches, there is not instituted by Christ any church more extensive or catholic entrusted with power for the administration of his ordinances, or the execution of any authority in his name.

7 A particular church gathered and completed according to the mind of Christ, consists of officers and members. The Lord Christ having given to his called ones (united according to his appointment in church-order) liberty and power to choose persons fitted by the Holy Ghost for that purpose, to be over them, and to minister to them in the Lord.

8 The members of these churches are saints by calling, visibly manifesting and evidencing (in and by their profession and walking) their obedience unto that call of Christ; who, being further known to each other by their confession of the faith wrought in them by the power of God, declared by themselves or otherwise manifested, do willingly consent to walk together according to the appointment of Christ; giving up themselves to the Lord, and to one another by the will of God in professed subjection to the ordinances of the gospel.

9 The officers appointed by Christ, to be chosen and set apart by the church so called, and gathered for the peculiar administration of ordinances, and execution of power and duty which he entrusts

them with, or calls them to, to be continued to the end of the world, are pastors, teachers, elders and deacons.

10 Churches thus gathered and assembling for the worship of God, are thereby visible and public, and their assemblies (in whatever place they are, according as they have liberty or opportunity) are therefore church or public assemblies.

11 The way appointed by Christ for the calling of any person, fitted and gifted by the Holy Ghost, unto the office of pastor, teacher or elder in a church, is, that he be chosen thereunto by the common suffrage of the church itself, and solemnly set apart by fasting and prayer, with imposition of hands of the eldership of that church, if there be any before constituted therein. And of a deacon, that he be chosen by the like suffrage, and set apart by prayer, and the like imposition of hands.

12 The essence of this call of a pastor, teacher or elder unto office, consists in the election of the church, together with his acceptation of it, and separation by fasting and prayer. And those who are so chosen, though not set apart by imposition of hands, are rightly constituted ministers of Jesus Christ, in whose name and authority they exercise the ministry to them so committed. The calling of deacons consisteth in the like election and acceptation with separation by prayer.

13 Although it be incumbent on the pastors and teachers of the churches to be instant in preaching the Word, by way of office; yet the work of preaching the Word is not so peculiarly confined to them, but that others also gifted and fitted by the Holy Ghost for it, and approved (being by lawful ways and means in the providence of God called thereunto) may publicly, ordinarily and constantly perform it; so that they give themselves up thereunto.

14 However, they who are engaged in the work of public preaching, and enjoy the public maintenance upon that account, are not thereby obliged to dispense the seals to any other than such as (being saints by calling, and gathered according to the

order of the gospel) they stand related to, as pastors or teachers. Yet ought they not to neglect others living within their parochial bounds, but besides their constant public preaching to them, they ought to enquire after their profiting by the Word, instructing them in, and pressing upon them (whether young or old) the great doctrines of the gospel, even personally and particularly, so far as their strength and time will admit.

15 Ordination alone without the election or precedent consent of the church, by those who formerly have been ordained by virtue of that power they have received by their ordination, doth not constitute any person a church-officer, or communicate office-power to him.

16 A church furnished with officers (according to the mind of Christ) hath full power to administer all his ordinances; and where there is want of any one or more officers required, that officer, or those which are in the church, may administer all the ordinances proper to their particular duty and offices; but where there are no teaching officers, none may administer the seals, nor can the church authorise any so to do.

17 In the carrying on of church-administrations, no person ought to be added to the church, but by the consent of the church itself; that so love (without dissimulation) may be preserved between all the members thereof.

18 Whereas the Lord Jesus Christ hath appointed and instituted as a means of edification, that those who walk not according to the rules and laws appointed by him (in respect of faith and life, so that just offence doth arise to the church thereby) be censured in his name and authority. Every church hath power in itself to exercise and execute all those censures appointed by him in the way and order prescribed in the gospel.

19 The censures so appointed by Christ, are admonition and excommunication. And whereas some offences are or may be known only to some, it is appointed by Christ, that those to

whom they are so known, do first admonish the offender in private: in public offences where any sin, before all. Or in case of non-amendment upon private admonition, the offence being related to the church, and the offender not manifesting his repentance, he is to be duly admonished in the name of Christ by the whole church, by the ministry of the elders of the church; and if this censure prevail not for his repentance, then he is to be cast out by excommunication with the consent of the church.

20 As all believers are bound to join themselves to particular churches, when and where they have opportunity so to do, so none are to be admitted unto the privileges of the churches, who do not submit themselves to the rule of Christ in the censures for the government of them.

21 This being the way prescribed by Christ in case of offence, no church-members upon any offences taken by them, having performed their duty required of them in this matter, ought to disturb any church-order, or absent themselves from the public assemblies, or the administration of any ordinances upon that pretence, but to wait upon Christ in the further proceeding of the church.

22 The power of censures being seated by Christ in a particular church, is to be exercised only towards particular members of each church respectively as such; and there is no power given by him unto any synods or ecclesiastical assemblies to excommunicate, or by their public edicts to threaten excommunication, or other church-censures against churches, magistrates, or their people upon any account, no man being obnoxious to that censure, but upon his personal miscarriage, as a member of a particular church.

23 Although the church is a society of men, assembling for the celebration of the ordinances according to the appointment of Christ, yet every society assembling for that end or purpose, upon the account of cohabitation within any civil precincts and

bounds, is not thereby constituted a church, seeing there may be wanting among them, what is essentially required thereunto; and therefore a believer living with others in such a precinct, may join himself with any church for his edification.

24 For the avoiding of differences that may otherwise arise, for the greater solemnity in the celebration of the ordinances of Christ, and the opening a way for the larger usefulness of the gifts and graces of the Holy Ghost; saints living in one city or town, or within such distances as that they may conveniently assemble for divine worship, ought rather to join in one church for their mutual strengthening and edification, than to set up many distinct societies.

25 As all churches and all the members of them are bound to pray continually for the good or prosperity of all the churches of Christ in all places, and upon all occasions to further it; (every one within the bounds of their places and callings, in the exercise of their gifts and graces). So the churches themselves (when planted by the providence of God, so as they may have opportunity and advantage for it) ought to hold communion amongst themselves for their peace, increase of love, and mutual edification.

26 In cases of difficulties or differences, either in point of doctrine or in administrations, wherein either the churches in general are concerned, or any one church in their peace, union, and edification, or any member or members of any church are injured in, or by any proceeding in censures, not agreeable to truth and order: it is according to the mind of Christ, that many churches holding communion together, do by their messengers meet in a synod or council, to consider and give their advice in, or about that matter in difference, to be reported to all the churches concerned. Howbeit, these synods so assembled are not entrusted with any church-power, properly so called, or with any jurisdiction over the churches themselves, to exercise

any censures, either over any churches or persons, or to impose their determinations on the churches or officers.

27 Besides these occasional synods or councils, there are not instituted by Christ any stated synods in a fixed combination of churches, or their officers in lesser or greater assemblies; nor are there any synods appointed by Christ in a way of subordination to one another.

28 Persons that are joined in church-fellowship, ought not lightly or without just cause to withdraw themselves from the communion of the church whereunto they are so joined. Nevertheless, where any person cannot continue in any church without his sin, either for want of the administration of any ordinances instituted by Christ, or by his being deprived of his due privileges, or compelled to anything in practice not warranted by the Word, or in case of persecution, or upon the account of conveniency of habitation; he consulting with the church, or the officer or officers thereof, may peaceably depart from the communion of the church, wherewith he hath so walked, to join himself with some other church, where he may enjoy the ordinances in the purity of the same, for his edification and consolation.

29 Such reforming churches as consist of persons sound in the faith and of conversation becoming the gospel, ought not to refuse the communion of each other, so far as may consist with their own principles respectively, though they walk not in all things according to the same rules of church-order.

30 Churches gathered and walking according to the mind of Christ, judging other churches (though less pure) to be true churches, may receive unto occasional communion with them, such members of those churches as are credibly testified to be godly, and live without offence.

*Appendix 2*

# THE 1833 DECLARATION OF FAITH

*Congregational Faith and Order*

# DECLARATION OF THE FAITH, CHURCH ORDER, AND DISCIPLINE OF THE CONGREGATIONAL, OR INDEPENDENT DISSENTERS,

## Adopted at the Annual Meeting of the Congregational Union, May 1833

The Congregational Churches in England and Wales, frequently called Independent, hold the following doctrines, as of Divine authority, and as the foundation of Christian faith and practice. They are also formed and governed according to the principles hereinafter stated.

# Preliminary Notes

1. It is not designed, in the following summary, to do more than to state the leading doctrines of faith and order maintained by Congregational Churches in general.

2. It is not proposed to offer any proofs, reasons, or arguments in support of the doctrines herein stated, but simply to declare what the Denomination believes to be taught by the pen of inspiration.

3. It is not intended to present a scholastic or critical confession of faith, but merely such a statement as any intelligent member of the body might offer, as containing its leading principles.

4. It is not intended that the following statement should be put forth with any authority, or as a standard to which assent should be required.

5. Disallowing the utility of creeds and articles of religion as a bond of union, and protesting against subscription to any human formularies as a term of communion, Congregationalists are yet willing to declare, for general information, what is commonly believed among them, reserving to every one the most perfect liberty of conscience.

6. Upon some minor points of doctrine and practice, they, differing among themselves, allow to each other the right to form an unbiased judgment of the Word of God.

7. They wish it to be observed, that, notwithstanding their jealousy of subscription to creeds and articles, and their disapproval of the imposition of any human standard, whether of faith or discipline, they are far more agreed in their doctrines and practices than any Church which enjoins subscription and enforces a human standard of orthodoxy; and they believe that there is no minister and no church among them that would deny the substance of any one of the following doctrines of religion, though each might prefer to state his sentiments in his own way.

## Principles of Religion

1. The Scriptures of the Old Testament, as received by the Jews, and the books of the New Testament, as received by the Primitive Christians from the Evangelists and Apostles, Congregational Churches believe to be Divinely inspired, and of supreme authority. These writings, in the languages in which they were originally composed, are to be consulted, with the aids of sound criticism, as a final appeal to all controversies, but the common version [at that time the Authorised Version (also known as the King James Version) of 1611] they consider to be adequate to the ordinary purposes or Christian instruction and edification.

2. They believe in one God, essentially wise, holy, just and good; eternal, infinite, and immutable in all natural and moral perfections; the Creator, Supporter, and Governor of all beings, and of all things.

3. They believe that God is revealed in the Scriptures, as the Father, the Son, and the Holy Spirit, and that to each are attributable the same Divine properties and perfections. The doctrine of the Divine existence, as above stated, they cordially believe, without attempting fully to explain.

4. They believe that man was created after the Divine image, sinless, and in his kind perfect.

5. They believe that the first man disobeyed the Divine command, fell from his state of innocence and purity, and involved all his posterity in the consequences of that fall.

6. They believe that, therefore, all mankind are born in sin, and that a fatal inclination to moral evil, utterly incurable by human means, is inherent in every descendant of Adam.

7. They believe that God having, before the foundation of the world, designed to redeem fallen man, made disclosures of his mercy, which were the grounds of faith and hope from the earliest ages.

8. They believe that God revealed more fully to Abraham the covenant of his grace, and, having promised that from his descendants should arise the Deliverer and Redeemer of mankind, set that patriarch and his posterity apart, as a race specially favoured and separated to his service; a peculiar church, formed and carefully preserved, under the Divine sanction and government until the birth of the promised Messiah.

9. They believe that, in the fullness of time, the Son of God was manifested in the flesh, being born of the Virgin Mary, but conceived by the power of the Holy Spirit; and that our Lord Jesus was both the Son of man and the Son of God; partaking fully and truly of human nature though without sin—equal with the Father and 'the express image of his person'.

10 They believe that Jesus Christ, the Son of God, revealed, either personally in his own ministry, or by the Holy Spirit in the ministry of his apostles, the whole mind of God, for our salvation; and that, by his obedience to the Divine law while he lived, and by his sufferings unto death, he meritoriously 'obtained eternal redemption for us'; having thereby vindicated and illustrated Divine justice, 'magnified the law', and brought in everlasting righteousness'.

11. They believe that, after his death and resurrection, he ascended up into heaven, where, as the Mediator, he 'ever liveth' to rule over all, and to 'make intercession for them that come unto God by him'.

12. They believe that the Holy Spirit is given, in consequence of Christ's mediation, to quicken and renew the hearts of men; and that his influence is indispensably necessary to bring a sinner to true repentance, to produce saving faith, to regenerate the heart, and to perfect our sanctification.

13. They believe that we are justified through faith in Christ, as 'the Lord our righteousness', and not 'by the works of the law'.

14. They believe that all who will be saved were the objects of God's eternal and electing love, and were given by an act of Divine sovereignty to the Son of God; which in no way interferes with the system of means, nor with the grounds of human responsibility; being wholly unrevealed as to its objects, and not a rule of human duty.

15. They believe that the Scriptures teach the final perseverance of all true believers to a state of eternal blessedness, which they are appointed to obtain through constant faith in Christ, and uniform obedience to his commands.

16. They believe that a holy life will be the necessary effect of a true faith and that good works are the certain fruits of a vital union to Christ.

17. They believe that the sanctification of true Christians, or their growth in the graces of the Spirit, and meetness for heaven, is gradually carried on through the whole period during which it pleases God to continue them in the present life, and that, at death, their souls, perfectly freed from all remains of evil, are immediately received into the presence of Christ.

18. They believe in the perpetual obligation of Baptism and the Lord's Supper; the former to be administered to all converts to Christianity and their children, by the application of water

to the subject, 'in the name of the Father, and of the Son, and of the Holy Ghost', and the latter to be celebrated by Christian churches as a token of faith in the Saviour, and of brotherly love.

19. They believe that Christ will finally come to judge the whole human race according to their works; that the bodies of the dead will be raised again; and that, as the Supreme Judge, he will divide the righteous from the wicked, will receive the righteous into 'life everlasting', but send away the wicked into 'everlasting punishment'.

20. They believe that Jesus Christ directed his followers to live together in Christian fellowship, and to maintain the communion of saints; and that, for this purpose, they are jointly to observe all Divine ordinances, and maintain that church order and discipline which is either expressly enjoined by inspired institution, or sanctioned by the undoubted example of the apostles and of apostolic churches.

## 2. Congregational Church Order and Discipline

1. The Congregational Churches hold it to be the will of Christ that true believers should voluntarily assemble together to observe religious ordinances, to promote mutual edification and holiness, to perpetuate and propagate the Gospel in the world, and to advance the glory and worship of God, through Jesus Christ; and that each society of believers, having these objects in view in its formation, is properly a Christian church.

2. They believe that the New Testament contains, either in the form of express statute, or in the example and practice of apostles and apostolic churches, all the articles of faith necessary to be believed, and all the principles of order and discipline requisite for constituting and governing Christian societies; and that human traditions, fathers and councils, canons and creeds, possess no authority over the faith and practice of Christians.

3. They acknowledge Christ as the only Head of the Church, and the officers of each church under him, as ordained to administer his laws impartially to all; and their only appeal, in all questions touching their religious faith and practice, is to the sacred Scriptures.

4. They believe that the New Testament authorises every Christian church to elect its own officers, to manage all its own affairs, and to stand independent of, and irresponsible to, all authority, saving that only of the Supreme and Divine Head of the Church, the Lord Jesus Christ.

5. They believe that the only officers placed by the Apostles over individual churches are the bishops or pastors and the deacons; the number of these being dependent upon the number of the church; and that to these, as the officers of the church, is committed respectively the administration of its spiritual and temporal concerns—subject, however, to the approbation of the church.

6. They believe that no persons should be received as members of Christian churches, but such as make a credible profession of Christianity, are living according to its precepts, and attest a willingness to be subject to its discipline, and that none should be excluded from the fellowship of the church, but such as deny the faith of Christ, violate his laws, or refuse to submit themselves to the discipline which the Word of God enforces.

7. The power of admission into any Christian church, and rejection from it, they believe to be vested in the church itself, and to be exercised only through the medium of its own officers.

8. They believe that Christian churches should stately meet for the celebration of public worship, for the observance of the Lord's supper, and for the sanctification of the first day of the week.

9. They believe that the power of a Christian church is purely spiritual and should in no way be corrupted by union with temporal or civil power.

10. They believe that it is the duty of Christian churches to hold communion with each other, to entertain an enlarged affection for each other, as members of the same body, and to co-operate for the promotion of the Christian cause; but that no church, or union of churches, has any right or power to interfere with the faith or discipline of any other church further than to separate from such as, in faith or practice, depart from the Gospel of Christ.

11. They believe that it is the privilege and duty of every church to call forth such of its members as may appear to be qualified by the Holy Spirit to sustain the office of the ministry; and that Christian churches unitedly ought to consider the maintenance of the Christian ministry in an adequate degree of learning as one of their especial cares, that the cause of the Gospel may be both honourably sustained and constantly promoted.

12. They believe that church officers, whether bishops or deacons, should be chosen by the free voice of the church; but that their dedication to the duties of their office should take place with special prayer, and by solemn designation, to which most of the churches add the imposition of hands by those already in office.

13. They believe that the fellowship of every Christian church should be so liberal as to admit to communion in the Lord's Supper all whose faith and godliness are, on the whole, undoubted, though conscientiously differing in points of minor importance and that this outward sign of fraternity in Christ should be co-extensive with the fraternity itself, though without involving any compliances which conscience would deem to be sinful.

# THE OBJECTS, BASIS OF FAITH, AND POLITY OF THE EVANGELICAL FELLOWSHIP OF CONGREGATIONAL CHURCHES

# THE EVANGELICAL FELLOWSHIP OF CONGREGATIONAL CHURCHES

## THE BEGINNINGS

With the ending of the Second World War, two Congregational ministers, Harland Brine and Gilbert Kirby, concerned at the spiritual decline of their denomination, felt led of God to begin a Congregational Evangelical Revival Fellowship. This Association, formed in 1947, was open to individual members of Congregational Churches and sought to witness to evangelical truth and to the need for Holy Spirit Revival in the Church.

A disregard of Scriptural authority had been evident for many years in the denomination and this was clearly shown in 1958, when the Congregational Union of England and Wales adopted a new Constitution and altered one of the Objects. Instead of 'to promote New Testament principles of Church fellowship and organisation' there was substituted the much vaguer 'to promote principles of church fellowship and organisation that are consonant with the Gospel'. At the same time a growing concern was being felt about the way in which the CUEW was both consolidating and centralising its power. In 1961, the Union published proposals for 'Covenant and Oversight' in the setting up of the Congregational Church in England and Wales. Three minister-members of the CERF, Gordon Booth, Edward Guest and David Marshall, were concerned at the prospect of oversight from a non-Scriptural organisation, and wrote to all brother ministers in the Fellowship inviting them to sign an Appeal to the Churches. Twenty seven ministers responded and the Appeal was sent out, calling upon Congregational Churches to stand firm on Scriptural principles.

With the setting up of the 'covenant body', it became evident that whole Churches were concerned to maintain an evangelical witness and, lest these Churches be left in isolation, the CERF Committee called a meeting of representatives of the Churches to wait on the Lord concerning the future. This resulted in the setting up of an Evangelical Fellowship of Congregational Churches (the name was changed to The Evangelical Fellowship of Congregational Churches in 1999). In April, 1967, joint meetings were held in Manchester and London and a Statement of evangelical doctrines was agreed. Later, a simple Constitution, necessary for legal and practical purposes, was approved.

## GOING ON

The Churches associated in EFCC are continuing Congregational Churches. They are evangelical and desire to have fellowship in Christ with all who love the Lord, honour his word, and preach the one true Gospel. They have formed the Evangelical Fellowship of Congregational Churches to provide a means of communication and an expression of Christian concern for one another. They have been shown again and again that 'the Lord will provide'. Prayers have been graciously answered, financial needs met, and ministers and Churches led to each other. The Bible has been proved anew in experience to be the inspired Word of God, and the Gospel proved to be the 'power of God unto salvation to everyone that believes'.

When the Fellowship was formed, concern was expressed lest it become hardened into a self-perpetuating Denomination and thus miss any call that the Lord might make for a wider grouping of Bible-believing Christians from all denominational backgrounds. Links in the Gospel have been established with evangelical Congregationalists in different parts of the world. The Fellowship is also in membership with the British Evangelical Council. This is a grouping of Churches, one in the fundamental doctrines of the faith and in a desire to discover and experience that true ecumenicity which the Scriptures certainly teach. Other bodies in the Council include the Free Church of Scotland, the Free Church of Scotland (Continuing), the Evangelical Presbyterian Church of Northern Ireland, the Fellowship of Independent Evangelical Churches, the Associating Evangelical Churches of Wales, two Associations of Strict Baptist Churches and the Congregational Union of Ireland.

## THE BASIS OF FELLOWSHIP

In order that the witness of the associated Churches may be clear, a Statement of Scriptural principles has been drawn up to act as a 'Basis of Fellowship'. This is not a creed we seek to impose upon others, but a testimony to what we ourselves believe. The foundation of the whole Basis is an acceptance of the Divine inspiration and supreme authority of the Bible, and if any statement therein can be shown to be unscriptural it will be corrected at once.

It is confidently asserted that this Basis of Fellowship, drawn as it is from the Scriptures, is thus fully in line with the truths declared in the Savoy Declaration of 1658, the Declaration of Principles at the formation of the Congregational Union of England and Wales in 1833, and with the original trust deeds of the vast majority of Congregational Churches.

## TRUST DEEDS

The safeguarding of its property is an important responsibility of any Church and, in view of the denominational changes which are taking place, Churches are advised to consider carefully the trusteeship of their property. Although this can be said to be purely a legal matter, it must surely be right that Churches are entitled to have trustees who are in sympathy with the position of continuing evangelical Congregationalists.

The Charity Commissioners can be expected to give full support to any Church which desires to remain truly Congregational. They do advise, however, that Churches should not remain in isolation but should link up with some such body as the Evangelical Fellowship of Congregational Churches. A memorandum giving simple advice on trust matters may be obtained from the Secretary of the Fellowship.

## FINANCIAL MATTERS

There are no membership fees. It is confidently expected that the Lord will provide for the needs of the Churches in fellowship through the generous giving of his people.

## CONSTITUTION OF THE EVANGELICAL FELLOWSHIP OF CONGREGATIONAL CHURCHES

(Adopted at the First Annual General Meeting held on Saturday, 5th June, 1971 at Bulstrode, Gerrards Cross, Buckinghamshire.) (With subsequent minor amendments)

### 1 The Objects of the Fellowship

To provide and promote fellowship between Evangelical Congregational Churches.

To advance Evangelical Christianity through Independent Churches.

To seek the welfare and express the faith and the true unity of the whole Church of Jesus Christ.

To bear witness to the Scriptural principles of the autonomy of the local Church and the freedom of believers in Christ.

To encourage prayer for the reviving power of the Holy Spirit in the Church.

To assist co-operation and counsel among the Churches with regard to such concerns as evangelism, missions, Church extension, ministry, and Christian action.

To enable Churches to share their resources, both spiritual and material.

To organise Conferences for prayer and fellowship, and for imparting information about the work of God in the Churches.

Provided always that the Fellowship is established for charitable purposes only, and this proviso shall be treated as over-riding the Objects set forth in this Clause.

## 2 (a) The Basis of Faith

### The Living God
God is Almighty, Eternal, and Unchanging. He is just and holy, gracious and merciful. He is the Maker and Ruler of all things and deserving of all praise and glory for ever.

### The Written Word
God's greatness and holiness are such that, without his aid, man can neither understand God nor find the way to a right relationship with him. In his mercy, however, God has made himself known. He has done this partially, through Creation, but explicitly through the Old and New Testaments of the Bible. We therefore accept all that was written in the Bible as not merely containing, but being, the inspired and infallible Word of God and the final and sufficient authority in all matters of Christian faith and life.

### The Trinity
God is one, existing through all eternity in three persons, Father, Son and Holy Spirit.

### The Sovereign God
God exercises sovereign power in Creation, Providence and Redemption.

### Man the Sinner
God created man perfect, but, after being tempted by the devil, man, by his own free choice, disobeyed God and became a sinner. Man's whole nature is now perverted by sin, and his fellowship with God is broken.

### Jesus the Saviour
God alone can deal with man's sin and bring about a reconciliation to himself. To achieve this, God became man in Jesus Christ. Jesus was conceived of the Holy Spirit and born of the Virgin Mary. He lived a sinless, human life and taught entirely without error. He suffered and died in the place of sinners, bearing their sin, and its guilt and punishment. He thus sets all believers free from the domination of the devil and the corruption of their own sinful nature, and removes from them, for ever, sin's lasting consequences.

### The Grace of God
God, in his grace, forgives and reconciles to himself all who turn to him in true repentance and who trust in Christ's atoning death. God imputes to them the righteousness of Christ himself, and adopts them as his own children.

### The Risen Lord
The Lord Jesus Christ was shown to be the Son of God by his miracles and by his bodily resurrection from the dead. He has ascended in power and glory to the presence of God, where he now pleads on behalf of those who call upon him in truth.

### The Holy Spirit
God the Holy Spirit must work in a man before he can enter into salvation. He leads the sinner into an awareness of his sinfulness, and brings him to repentance and trust in Christ. He

brings to birth in him a new and eternal life, and, by his continuing work, develops in this new life the fruits of love and holiness.

## The Second Coming
God is bringing all human history to a climax which will be marked by the visible return to the earth of the Lord Jesus Christ.

## Jesus the Judge
God has appointed Jesus as Judge and there will be a final judgment. Those who are saved will be raised in a glorified body and enjoy eternally and to the full the presence of their Lord. Those who have rejected Christ will be banished from God for ever.

## The One Church
All who have been redeemed with the precious blood of Christ, and upon whom God has bestowed his righteousness as a free gift belong to Christ. They alone may rightly be called Christians. They alone are members of the one universal and eternal Church of Christ.

## The Gathered Church
Each local Church is a fellowship of believers gathered by Christ, and has no need of, nor should acknowledge, any other authority than his. Through him, it has direct access to God and enjoys fellowship with other assemblies of his people in a unity which transcends all barriers.

## 2 (b) Church Polity
We believe that Jesus Christ is the Head of the Church universal, which is his body, and of each local Church.

We believe that each local Church is in itself a complete Church, therefore autonomous, possessing all the rights and responsibilities of the Church by the Holy Spirit as set forth in the Scriptures.

We believe that Jesus Christ exercises his authority in each local Church by the Holy Spirit and through the Scriptures.

We believe that each local Church, through its Church Meeting, is answerable only to Jesus Christ, and not to any association, conference, council, synod, or any other ecclesiastical body.

We believe it is proper and beneficial for each local Church to seek fellowship and counsel of other Churches that are like-minded in the Lord.

**Note:** The Fellowship accepts the earlier formulations of faith contained in the Savoy Declaration of 1658 and the Declaration of Principles at the formation of the Congregational Union of England and Wales in 1833 as valuable guide-lines, without them necessarily being of binding effect.

### 3 Membership

(a) Membership is open to Congregational or Independent Churches which annually signify in writing their agreement with the Objects, Basis of Faith and Polity.

(b) Associate membership is open to Churches accepting the Basis of Faith, but whose denominational attachments are not yet clearly determined.

(c) Personal membership is open to any person being in membership of a local church who accepts the Objects, Basis of Faith and Polity of the Fellowship and who pays an annual subscription as set by the committee. Such persons would be entitled to attend the Annual General Meeting (but would have no voting rights) and would receive *Concern* and *Prayer Concern*.

### 4 Annual Meetings

An Annual General Meeting of the Fellowship shall be held once in each year such Meeting being held not later than eighteen months after the previous Meeting. Twenty-eight days' notice of the Meeting shall be sent by the Secretary to all member Churches, who shall be invited to send a representative or representatives to the Meeting. Ten member Churches represented shall form a quorum.

## 5 Special Meetings

A Special Meeting of the Fellowship may be called at any time by the Committee of the Fellowship, or by not fewer than five member Churches of the Fellowship on addressing a letter to the Secretary stating the object of the Meeting. The Secretary shall thereupon give not less than twenty-eight days' notice of the Meeting to all member Churches, who shall be invited to send a representative or representatives to the Meeting. Ten member Churches represented shall form a quorum.

## 6 Voting

All member Churches shall have the right to vote by two representatives at Annual General Meetings and Special Meetings of the Fellowship. All issues shall be decided on a simply majority, with every member Church having a maximum of two votes.

## 7 Finance

A Statement of Accounts of the Fellowship, prepared by the Treasurer and duly audited by two persons appointed by the Annual General Meeting, shall be circulated to all member Churches with the Agenda for the following Annual General Meeting. No formal subscriptions are charged to members.

## 8 The Committee

(a) The Fellowship shall be served by a Committee, composed of not less than ten and not more than twenty persons.

One third, or the number nearest to one third, of the members of the Committee shall retire annually at the Annual General Meeting but shall be eligible for re-election. The members to retire shall be those who have been longest in office since their last election. As between members of equal seniority those to retire shall in the absence of agreement be determined by lot.

Persons to serve on the Committee shall (a) be members of Churches in the Fellowship and (b) must signify in writing their agreement with the Objects and Basis of Faith of the Fellowship. Such persons shall be nominated for election by one or more member Churches of the Fellowship.

The names and relevant particulars of persons so nominated must be in the hands of the Secretary by January 31st prior to the Annual General Meeting of that year.

Election shall be by postal ballot under arrangements made by the Secretary and the result shall be declared at the Annual General Meeting. No person receiving less than ten votes shall be deemed to be elected.

(b) The Committee shall have power to co-opt to itself not more than three persons who signify in writing their agreement with the Objects and Basis of Faith. Such persons shall retire annually but may be co-opted again for further service.

(c) The Committee shall elect from its members a Chairman, Secretary, Treasurer, and Editor of the Fellowship magazine. The Chairman so elected shall also act as chairman at the Annual General and Special Meetings of the Fellowship.

(d) The Committee may also meet for the despatch of business, adjourn, and otherwise regulate its proceedings as it thinks fit. The quorum for the transaction of business shall be five. The Committee will strive for unanimity, but any matters within its province may be decided by a two-thirds majority of votes of the members of the Committee present and voting at that Meeting.

(e) The Secretary shall give notice in writing to all members of the Committee concerning the calling of meetings.

(f) The Committee may be assisted by Sub-Committees, consisting of one or more of its members and of such other persons as shall signify in writing their full and active agreement with the Objects and Basis of Faith of the Fellowship. Such Sub-Committees shall conform to any directions imposed on them by the Committee as to the conduct of their proceedings.

(g) If a Committee fails to obtain a quorum, any urgent Resolution in writing, signed by all members of the Committee, shall be valid and effectual as a Resolution passed at a meeting duly convened and held.

(h) The Committee shall have power to employ a paid officer or officers to serve the Fellowship upon such terms as the Committee shall think fit.

(i) Members of the Committee shall not be entitled to remuneration but shall be entitled to be paid all travelling and other expenses properly incurred in the execution of their duties.

## 9 Alteration of Constitution

No part of the Objects or Basis of Faith or of the Constitution of the Fellowship shall be repealed, altered, or added to, except at a Special Meeting in notice whereof the proposed changes shall have been set forth. No changes shall be made without a three-quarters majority.

This Clause shall also apply to any Resolution to wind up the Fellowship.

## 10 Property

The Committee shall vest the property and funds of the Fellowship in not fewer than two nor more than four individual trustees or in a trust corporation. Individual trustees must on appointment be members of the Committee. In the event of a trustee retiring or resigning from membership of the Committee, or failing to gain re-election at any succeeding Annual General Meeting, such trustee shall be deemed *ipso facto* to have resigned his trusteeship at the date of his retirement, resignation, or failure to gain re-election whichever the case may be, and shall upon request transfer any property standing in his name in accordance with the directions of the continuing trustees. New trustees shall be appointed as and when necessary by the Committee.

## 11 Winding up

If upon the winding up or dissolution of the Fellowship there remains, after the satisfaction of all its debts and liabilities, any property whatsoever, the same shall be distributed among the member churches (being charities) of the Fellowship at the date of dissolution in equal shares.

# Books on Congregational Principles Available from EFCC

**Telling Another Generation** ed. Mike Plant and Alan Tovey
This book contains a symposium of papers originally written to mark the twenty-fifth anniversary of EFCC, and as a tribute to Stan Guest, who has been closely involved in the work of EFCC ever since its formation, and retired as secretary of the Fellowship in 1989.

**Serving as a Deacon** by John Legg
Now reprinted in a revised edition. 'Diaconates might find it useful to supply each member with a copy of this work'—*Evangelicals Now.*

**Children of the Covenant** by John Legg
The biblical basis for infant baptism.

**Signs and Seals of the Covenant** by CG Kirkby
A biblical review of the doctrine of Christian baptism.

**Wandering Pilgrims** by ES Guest
Subtitled *Whatever Happened to the Congregational Churches?* A brief history of Congregational, examining the reasons for Congregationalism's decline in the 20th century.

**Manual of Congregational Principles** by RW Dale
The definitive work of Congregational church government.

**Christian Fellowship or the Church Member's Guide** by John Angell James
A practical manual for church members to learn their duties and responsibilities.

**Visible Saints: The Congregational Way: 1640–1660** by Geoffrey F. Nuttall
A scholarly examination of the exciting period of English church history when the practicalities of Congregational principles were worked out in detail.